D0376955

SONG
& Silence

SONG
& Silence

Voicing the Soul

In the Spirit of Song

Susan Elizabeth Hale

Susan Elizabeth Hale

La Alameda Press
Albuquerque • New Mexico

Acknowledgments

This book would not have come into being without J.B. Bryan hearing its heartbeat and singing it to life. I would also like to thank Jimalee Gordon who edited the book and gave invaluable suggestions; my apprentice Peggy Allen for her labor of love in proofing, correcting copy and helping with transitions in the early chapters; my husband David for his constant love and support for my song path; John Stokes for the Foreword and adding to my understanding of the Songlines; Danny Shanahan for one of my favorite cartoons; Marc Schevené for being in the right place at the right time, Renee Printz, Donna Hanna Chase, Don Chase, Betsy Kuhn, Carolynne Colby-Schmeltzer, Achmed, Bill Georgevich and Paul Thill for reading, proofing, typing and adding their special touches; Jenny Kim, Norma Jean Wilkes, Fran A'Hearn Smith and Judith Park who all read the early draft of the book and gave me needed feedback; Forrest Evans, Joseph Rael, Marshall Smith, Brett Nelson, Thomas Williams, Paul Marcus and the men in my poetry group for input on Men's Voices; Betsy James, Valentina de Cruz-Dixon, Shoshona Blankman, Angelique Cook-Wilcox and Judith Roderick for emotional support when I felt like a pregnant whale; Sandia Mountain and the forest near my home for grounding, beauty and inspiration; and especially to the members of the Wednesday night toning group and all my students and clients whose voices sing in these pages.

ISBN 0~9631909~3~8

La Alameda Press
9636 Guadalupe Trail NW
Albuquerque, New Mexico 87114

For my Mother
who sang to me

“Breath is the infinite self, the voice.
There is an eternal perception
of a beautiful journey
that is ever unfolding,
and that comes from the breath.
So, for a singer who is singing—
the very act of breathing:
inhalation and exhalation—
is doing what God is doing
in the process of creating everything
we know on this plane.”

JOSEPH RAEL

Contents

Foreword
by John Stokes

One evening in Moscow, Mr. G.I. Gurdjieff was emphasizing to a student the Unity of the Laws of the Universe. He asked the man to choose "something of regular structure" that he might use as a vehicle for his explanation. The student chose the musical scale.

"You have made a good choice," said Gurdjieff. He noted that the musical scale in its present form had been constructed in ancient time by those possessed of great knowledge. Of particular interest were the gaps which exist in every octave between the notes *mi* and *fa* and also *ti* of one octave and *do* of the next. As Gurdjieff explained— the fundamental octaves send forth secondary octaves at these points, much like the formation of a tree. From the trunk or main octave, boughs branch out, producing in turn small branches and twigs. Then leaves appear and within them, the veins begin to form.

He then compared the human body to a three-storied factory, the stories representing the head, chest and abdomen. Taken together, the body is a fundamental octave. Each story is a secondary octave, each receiving "food" of a suitable nature from outside which it assimilates— the abdomen takes in food and drink, the chest takes in air, and the head takes in "impressions." The energy generated by each story is converted through a series of steps and half-steps which enable it to be utilized by the next story. "You see," Gurdjieff went on, "that he who possesses a full and complete understanding of the system of octaves, as it might be called, possesses the key to understanding of Unity…" [1]

This notion that sound and silence are fundamental to an understanding of life on Earth is not restricted to one people or even one continent. Whether in the form of a word, a song, a sound or a sacred formula, this truth is found in creation stories from around the world. For instance, in the Hopi creation tales, Spider Woman creates the two twins— Pöqanghoya and Palöngawhoya— to help her bring sound and movement to the First World. (For what is life without movement and sound?) She instructs the twin on the left, Palöngawhoya, to help keep this world in order by sending out a sound that may be heard throughout the land. Traveling along the earth's axis from pole to pole, Palöngawhoya resounds his call, "turning the whole world into an instrument of sound, and sound into an instrument" for carrying messages of praise to the Creator. In this way, everything was tuned to the Creator's voice. Then the human body was constructed in the same way as the earth, with the backbone as the axis and several vibratory centers (like the yogic *chakras*) along this axis which echoed the primordial sound of life throughout the universe.[2]

So, it would seem that this earth and all of the life upon it and around it can be understood in terms of sound alone. Perhaps this is the true meaning of *Universe*— one line, one song, one turning. We are each just singing our part in this great natural concerto. In fact, Gary Snyder and Lewis Thomas (a poet and a biologist) are among those who wonder whether the steady flow of energy from the sun is "mathematically" destined to cause matter to arrange itself symmetrically into an increasingly ordered state. Then could it be that "the rhythm of insects, the long pulsing runs of bird songs, the descants of whales, the modulated vibrations of millions of locusts in migration" are the sounds which represent this process?[3]

In 1984, saxophonist Paul Winter invited me to accompany him on a musical whalewatch off the coast of Massachusetts. Several miles offshore two humpbacked whales appeared in the distance and Paul used the high notes of his soprano sax to call them closer. I joined him on the didjeridu and the whales began to dance to our music, sometimes in stereo with a whale on either side of our boat. This wasn't Sea World, these whales weren't trained. This was out in the open ocean! The whales danced for our boatload of 350 people for more than four hours. After some songs, they would roll over on their backs and clap their flippers. Certain songs on the didjeridu made the whales stop and smack their tales on the surface. Sometimes they would pull up alongside the boat and trumpet through their blowholes, sounding almost like an elephant.

During all of this, the crowd was laughing and screaming in amazement. After four hours, everyone's film was gone, the video tape used up, our voices spent, my lips were completely spent. They were split and bleeding from playing so hard for so long. But the whales were still dancing, as if to say— "C'mon. What's wrong? Can't keep up? C'mon. Be high like us!" It was fantastic.

Back on land, Paul took me into his studio. He wanted me to hear something. He got out a variable speed tape deck. He put on a tape of a bird song and then slowed it down more than half its normal speed. It sounded just like a humpbacked whale. Then he put on a tape of whales singing and cranked it up fast— this sounded just like a meadowlark! I still get goosebumps when I think of that whalewatch.

I use music as my model for energy in this world. Paul Winter would call it "common ground." This idea of sound and energy goes back to the Aboriginal Australian view that we actually sing the world into being and that these songs are maps that describe the world and let us know where we are in it. Through singing we return to that original creative time when the world was sung into existence from the potential energies within the earth. It's important to remember that this creative time— the Dreamtime— is not a moment in the distant past. It is the Eternal Present, this moment like no other. An opportunity to join in song with the whales, the birds, the Sun. Why do some people remember this while others have forgotten? An interesting question.

How can we get back to knowing this? An even more interesting question and one that might take us the rest of our life to answer. To help us find our voice, Susan Hale has brought together her thoughts, her work and experienced investigations on song and silence in a way that I hope will open the reader to the power of song. As she notes in her Preface, we all have a song but many of us have lost touch with this essential part of our lives. Singing is at the root of all spiritual practice. And what is spiritual practice but the process of becoming fully human? Song possesses the gentle power of dispersion that can break up and dissolve blockages when our vital energies are jammed up inside. Like the celebrations of old which used song and ceremony to gather people together and arouse a strong tide of emotion that was shared by all hearts in unison, singing can bring us back into harmony with our own humanness. After all, the whales are waiting for us to sing our part.

Corrales, New Mexico

1. G.I. Gurdjieff, *Views from the Real World: Early Talks of Gurdjieff,* Dutton, New York, 1973, pp. 17-20.
2. Frank Waters, *Book of the Hopi*, Penguin Books, Middlesex, England, 1963, p. 3-27.
3. Lewis Thomas quoted by Gary Snyder, *The Old Ways,* City Lights, San Francisco, 40077, p. 41.

Preface

Everyone has a song.
But many people have lost touch with this
vital part of their being. Perhaps you are one of them.
This book shares experiential truths and lessons
of the healing power of sound, song and silence
learned in the years of my own journey as a singer.
It explores my work as a music therapist
and the journeys of my clients.
This is not a clinical music therapy book nor an
academic research project, although there are clinical
examples and references from many books.
Rather, this book weaves reflections about the voice,
personal experiences, questions about 20th century
America and how singing has become a
diminished priority in people's daily lives.
In this book I show how song reaches beneath
the cultural matrix of any particular group
and connects us with Nature and each other
in meaningful ways. I hope that each person
reading this book can listen for his or her voice
and begin to sing.

THIS
Book
creates
the image
of a
song journey
that starts
with
my own path
and is
structured
as *a song*
with an
introduction,
three verses,
a chorus
and
a refrain.

My Song Journey

"All my being is song. I sing as I draw my breath."
Orpingalik (Eskimo)

My journey through song began as a baby. My Mother said I sang the first few notes to "Rock-a-bye Baby" before I talked. I have been singing ever since. My Mother sang to me often. I remember her songs. She sang in a trio in the 1930's and 40's— so, instead of the standard lullabies I heard *"Somewhere Over the Rainbow," "I'll Be With You in Apple Blossom Time,"* and *"Bongo, Bongo, Bongo I Don't Wanna Leave the Congo."* Singing was a life-line connecting myself, my Mother and the world. It was a soothing beautiful language that spoke of feelings and the magic of a place "where troubles melt like lemon drops."[1]

I remember that as a three and four year-old the teenagers at my church egged me to go up on stage and sing. At my brother's Cub Scout meetings I sang *"God Bless America"* along with others in a falsetto soprano, trying to imitate Jeannette McDonald. Riding in the car my mother, brother and I would sing *"Catch a Falling Star and Put It in Your Pocket"* in three-part harmony.

I grew up with a diverse exposure to music. My mother loved opera and musical theatre. My brother played piano, oboe and clarinet. He played Bach and Chopin on the piano, but liked to listen to Stravinsky and Shostakovich. My dad enjoyed Big Band music and cowboy songs. My brother played the piano while we sang songs from Gilbert and Sullivan's *"Mikado"* or from The Reader's Digest Treasury of Songs . At Christmas my mother always sang in The Messiah. My favorite Christmas memories were the Christmas Eve services when we sang carols by candlelight.

As a teenager I went to San Francisco to see "The Fantastiks" and pretended I was Louisa, one of the main characters. I sang along with my girlfriends to Peter, Paul and Mary, Joan Baez, Judy Collins, Buffy St. Marie and Barbra Streisand. As my interest in folk music grew, I got together with friends to sing. We formed a group called *The Illegitimate Jug Band* and sang at a hootenanny at a local junior college.

I moved to northern California in the late 60's and attended the Big Sur Folk Festival where I heard Joan Baez sing *"Amazing Grace"* a capella. Her voice echoed through the canyon and made a powerful impression upon me. While attending college, I went Sufi Dancing and learned Zikrs and chants. I drove to San Francisco to the House of Love and Prayer whenever Rabbi Schlomo Carlbach was in town and would be mesmerized by his wordless songs and storytelling. In my Yoga class we sang Sanskrit chants. I learned many chants at women's moon circles.

Even though I sang all the time, I was aware that I couldn't burst out in song whenever I wanted to. I noticed that most people didn't sing. On trips when I sang in the car I would notice the radio would get turned on automatically. I also grew up with many messages, both familial and societal, that I was too sensitive and too emotional. I began to equate these qualities with singing. So I learned to sing alone, in choirs, while performing, or in special "singing zones" like Sufi Dancing.

I learned that most of the world was a "no singing zone." The only time I heard people sing to each other in public was either in bars or singing *"Happy Birthday"*, usually with some degree of embarassment.

After graduating with a BA in psychology and special education, I studied music therapy at the University of Kansas. I sang in choirs, chamber groups and collegium musicum ensembles. I took voice lessons and loved the French art songs of Faure, Debussy and Ravel.

As a music therapy student I needed to do fifteen performances, so I sang at local cafes and senior centers. I loved singing to people, but when it was time for my senior recital I knew the meaning of nervousness. From attending student recitals, I often heard the voices of peers criticizing other students in stuffy tones. The natural joy of singing was stifled in this atmosphere. This wasn't due to the songs themselves, but to the attitudes of perfectionism and rivalry that were bred in the music conservatory.

After I graduated and worked as a music therapist, I began to notice a sneering attitude which many people had towards singing. When I led singing sessions in a psychiatric unit, the patients and doctors in the addictions unit laughed at us. I began to notice a social embarassment around singing. The attitudes were stifling. In the same hospital, I presented my observations at a case conference for a woman I'd worked with in music therapy. She had written a beautiful song of self-affirmation. She was near discharge and said that when she left the hospital she wanted to sing this song as she walked out of the hospital doors into the outside world for the first time in three months. I saw this as an empowering ritual. But as I told the story one of the doctors snickered and said, "then we'll know she's really crazy." This was received by this "professional" staff with a chorus of laughter. What is it about singing that makes people so nervous? What is it about singing that is "crazy"?

I eventually quit working in hospitals and started a private practice. While living in New Mexico I began leading workshops called *Circle the Earth with Song.* At these workshops I taught different chants which I had collected from around the world, as well as some original chants of my own. I created a tape with the same title to inspire others to sing.

In 1986 I attended a *Seeds of Singing* workshop with Susan Osborn, a recording artist who had been the lead singer for the *Paul Winter Consort.* For years I had sung along with her on recordings and now I would have an opportunity to hear her in person and to sing with her. Even though I was familiar with some of her "techniques" from my music therapy background, I was unprepared for the effect her voice and presence would have on me. Susan sang from a deep well inside her soul. She sang wordless songs riding on her outbreath which vibrated throughout the room. She sang her truth in the moment. It was as if she was a faith healer in song. Her voice touched a deep chord in my being that has been vibrating ever since. For the first time I truly experienced not only my own need to sing but the human need to sing. I knew we had gotten very far away from this type of soul-singing. I had two more opportunities to work with Susan and deepen the voicing of my soul. Each time I sang I unearthed another layer of my voice. Each time that I took a risk to go into the center of the circle and breathe in and let my song emerge, I felt in touch with a greater life-force moving through me. Breathing in and allowing life to move through me in tones was exhilarating. As I sang I was witnessed by a circle of other singers— this was empowering. Hearing the audible transformation in peoples' voices was moving.

My evening gatherings grew into six-week *Joy of Singing* classes. I took every opportunity I could to work with others exploring this sound terrain. Sarah Benson, Jill Purce, Vickie Dodd, Helen Bonny, Kay Gardner and Ysaye Barnwell (from *Sweet Honey in the Rock*) were some of the teachers who inspired me. Each one has added to my understanding of the voice and the power of song. I learned new chants and ways of singing and praying through song at womens' gatherings throughout New Mexico. I read everything I could find about the voice.

In the mornings I meditated with overtone chanting and other sound practices, noting the results which I felt in my voice, body and psyche. When a book gave a vocal practice I would sing with it over time to see if it did what it said it would.

I began to specialize in my private practice in helping people find their voices. With very few exceptions the ones who have found their way into my office have been women. These students and clients have continued to teach me how sensitive the voice is to criticism and abuse, and how ready it is to blossom when given a safe atmosphere of encouragement. Before we can find our voices we have to trust that we are worth listening to and that we will be heard.

Through toning I have learned to listen inside myself and voice what I hear. This is a constant act of listening and risking to expose and make audible what I feel in the moment. As I worked with clients, I began to further sensitize my inner hearing to the unexpressed sounds inside waiting to be heard. When a client would get stuck in fear, not being able to make her own sound I sometimes asked, "May I give voice to what I'm hearing?" As I made the sounds, I heard clients report that something moved inside . . . memories, emotions, physical sensations . . . that moved through the block and helped them to express their own sounds. Something resonated in them.

Rather than singing a client's sounds, I feel that what I am doing is vocally expressing my human response to their pain. Often the sounds of distress surface first and are followed by more pure tones that bring harmony. This is not a cure but a way to help people back to their patterns of wholeness.

As I worked with women with vocal blocks I began to see this more and more as a political and social issue, rather than a personal one. I could see and hear the psychological reasons for the vocal blocks, and I also began to see a social context. A woman having a voice in the world is a political issue. If we can't know and give voice to our innermost selves then we risk being controlled by those with the strongest voice which, in our society usually means rich, white men. We are not encouraged as women to know ourselves. We are encouraged to fit into someone else's idea of who we should be, rather than to discover and express our unique gifts. Vocal women get labeled pushy, bitchy, uppity, hostile. Emotions are not encouraged. Intuition is not encouraged. Spirituality outside of organized religion is not encouraged. What a woman knows is often not articulated. Over the past 20 years I have heard women in women's groups say similar things: "I don't know how to talk about what we do here" or "I don't have any words for my experience." We do know how to talk, but it is often not in a logical mode. When women get together we talk about our inner experiences. We talk in emotional, image-laden words. Women's words blossom with encouragement and close listening. But, since the "real" world doesn't talk this way, we silence ourselves at work or at home because we're afraid of being criticized, misunderstood or ignored. So we don't give our uniquely feminine gifts to the world. To have a voice is to have power in the world. I've seen how, when a woman opens her voice to sing her truth, it carries over into her daily life. She can take a stand to speak her truth, to know who she is, what she thinks, and what she feels.

This view has led me into environmental causes. Most primal cultures view the earth as female, the womb/tomb from which all life emerges and where we will finally rest. The earth is speaking to us in many ways and we're not listening. Rather than taking the time to listen to the breeze, the trees and the rocks, people often listen to the radio or conversations about work when they go to nature. Every living thing has its unique vibrational pattern that can be felt and heard if the time is taken to listen. From these interests I began to lead *Sing for the Earth* workshops where we find our own place on the earth and listen for the songs and poems we hear. The Western mind may see this as further "craziness" but the primal mind understands. Willy Whitefeather, a Cherokee man, says:

> *"Stones are like lonely old people, standing and waiting to be sung to. Our people have always sung songs of admiration to the qualities of strength, beauty and endurance that stones bring to the world . . . they are tired and lonely now because the white world has become so blind and selfish. They live in a hollow unsung world."* [2]

My mission is to help people find their voices, to give voice to the feminine, and to sensitize people to their natural world so that we can co-create a world in which we can fully embrace our diversity, imagination, gifts and creativity. We need a world in which we can sing and be heard. We need to listen to each other much more fully.

I emphasize the feminine in this book, not because it is the only voice to be heard, many men also struggle with these same issues, but because most of my clients and students are women. As a woman I know the power of emotion, the power of intuition, the power of memory, the power of compassion, the power of the body's knowledge, and the power within the womb. These do belong to the feminine realm, whether inside a man or a woman. The power has been denigrated or ignored. I believe that before a greater global renewal can occur the world needs to hear the power of the feminine voice in all its depth and fullness.

This is my song journey. I encourage you to begin your own. Take a moment to listen to the silence.

Opening quote: Orpingalik, in Joan Halifax's *Shamanic Voices*, E.P. Dutton, New York, 1979, p. 32.

1. E. Y. Harburg and Harold Arlen, "Somewhere Over The Rainbow" from *The Wizard of Oz*, Metro-Goldwyn-Mayer Inc., New York, 1938.
2. Robert Lawlor, *Voices of the First Day: Awakenings in Aboriginal Dreamtime*, Inner Traditions, Rochester, Vermont, 1991, p. 41.

Introduction

Song

"In Latin the term 'personare' means 'to sound through something.' Thus, at the base of the concept of the person (the concept of that which really makes a human being an unmistakable, singular per-sonality) stands the concept of sound: 'through the tone.' If nothing sounds through from the bottom of the being, a human being is human biologically, at best, but is not a per-son, because he does not live through the son (the tone, the sound). He does not live the sound which is the world."
Joachim-Ernst Berendt

Within each of us a true voice carries the radiance of our humanity. This voice contains our deepest feelings, our spiritual longings, our hopes, fears and personal truths. Each voice speaks uniquely. Each needs to be heard. Such voices need to emerge from the numbing of our techno-crazed lives so that a healing in our relationship to Nature can take place. We need our voices for this personal and collective healing. We need to create environments in which we listen to each other— not to impress with pretty sounds or speeches, but to allow the truth of our lives to be heard. How do we find our true voices? How do we listen? What is singing?

Orpingalik, an Eskimo shaman, answers that "songs are thoughts, sung with the breath when people are moved by great forces, and ordinary speech no longer suffices."[1] Singing is the most personalized form of musical expression. It involves the diaphragm, chest, heart, lungs, throat, tongue, face — the exposed frontal part of our bodies where our deepest emotions are stored. When we sing we become a resonator, an instrument, vibrating with the beauty of tone. We feel song vibrate through our entire system, linking body, mind, emotion, soul and spirit.

Singing and emotion are closely related. With our life's breath we are moved to sing. Singing is a basic response to our environment. Who can imagine a world without the sound of laughter, the cooing of babies, the wailing of grief? Even before they spoke, our ancestors took the leap from these utterances to singing. Some speculate that song preceded speech and that the first speech was akin to the sing-song way mothers instinctively talk to babies. Song is an intrinsic part of our human heritage. For this reason, I believe singing is essential to our most basic human needs.

In my workshops I asked over 100 participants to respond to a questionaire regarding attitudes about singing. Here is a summary of their responses when asked to define singing:

SINGING is —

a way to express feelings
an expression of the soul
a celebration of life
freeing
healing

Song

essential
good for the soul
one of humankind's highest endeavors
the best form of getting emotions through to others
communication
fun

The benefits of singing are many.
On a physical level singing:

pushes stale air out of the body
brings in new air which moves oxygen and nutrients to cells
relaxes and loosens the jaw muscles
reduces stress
creates a unique and gentle vibration in the brain
stimulating circulation and removing waste
improves circulation of oxygen and nutrients
stimulates the internal organs
releases tension in the diaphragm
energizes and relaxes the body

On an emotional level singing:

lessens anxiety
relieves depression
gets one in touch with emotions
releases emotions
changes moods

On a psychological level singing:

clears mental clutter
increases self-esteem
eases loneliness
uplifts the mind
allows for integration

On a spiritual level singing:
touches the soul
assists in meditation
connects one with the inner self
aids in prayer
On a social level singing:
creates intimacy
brings people together
conveys important messages
allows for communication without words

With so many benefits why isn't singing a daily part of life? The fears that prevent us from singing are many:
"My voice isn't good enough."
"I don't want others to dislike me."
"People will be repelled if I sing."
"I don't want to be judged."
"I might forget the words or the tune."
"I might stick out."
In short— "What will people think?"

When I talk about singing I speak of it in a primal sense rather than following the notes in a songbook. What does it mean to really sing? When we sing— we feel sound pulsing through the body in a way that connects us to something greater than ourselves. The song moves through the body and moves others in a tangible way.

"Voice is a mystery.
Containing in a breath instantly lost,

Song

Everything that is the person.
One's signature, written on air
But heard as genuine
By an authentic listener."[2]

This type of singing *can* occur when singing a composed song. However, until a person has explored his or her emotional depth, and married it with technique, singing can be a surface affair. Bernice Johnson Reagon speaks to this point. She says her students would give her "melody, harmony, rhythm and style, and I kept asking for the rest. I wanted to feel and hear their soul in their singing. The talk of older women in church kept coming back to me as a standard, 'The child's got a nice voice but I don't feel nothing.' To sing and not use it to reveal and work over some aspect of one's internal condition is to miss a major opportunity to bring strength and peace into one's life. I wanted my students to be able to walk this way of singing, to have a way to change their spiritual, physical, and emotional condition by running sound through their bodies."[3] How do we find a way to run sound through our bodies? This book shows you how. Though songs as we recognize them can be found in these pages, most of the examples come from wordless songs created in the moment from deep inward listening. This is described as *toning*, which I believe to be the foundation for finding one's voice. Toning is a connection to our archaic tribal roots, regardless of which culture we belong to.

Throughout this book I give many examples of toning. There have been many influences throughout the years that have taught me about toning. Some of these include Laurel Elizabeth Keye's book, Toning, her tapes and workshops; Susan Osborn's wonderful *Seeds of Singing* workshops; and my own experimentation with voice— by myself and with my students.

What is toning? I use toning as a way of honoring the unique voice of each person. It is a way of listening deeply to one's self at any given moment and voicing what is heard inside. In a group we listen to ourselves and others and respond with a collective voice— we sing our own truth and the truth of what we hear in others. Toning acknowledges our humanity— the pains, frustrations and joys of our lives and lets them live through sound. When we tone we say— "Listen! This is me! This is how I feel! "

Toning allows us to be part of something greater, to open up so that Spirit can sing through us. It is a way of voicing the soul. Two of my clients have said: "Toning is like a spectrum of colors" and "toning goes straight to my core."

To tone—

breathe in through your nose and out through your mouth... listen to the silence... listen to the natural sounds of your outbreath... allow the breath to be like a river that supports your sounds as they emerge... as you continue to breathe in this way allow yourself to sigh, yawn or groan... listen for what sounds want to be voiced... continue to sigh or groan and as you continue, allow a tone to ride on the outbreath... perhaps you will feel like toning on one note... perhaps you will find your voice moving down or up and down... listen to where your voice wants to be... feel the sounds vibrating in your body... the breathing in is just as important as the toning... the silence is just as important as the song... breathing in is the time of listening... breathing out is the time for your voice to be heard, perhaps by others, perhaps by yourself... resist the temptation to judge or analyze your sounds... let

> them be what they are... tell your inner critic to go on vacation so you can have this experience of breath and tone... continue toning as long as you feel the impulse... as you finish allow yourself to sit in silence for a few moments to feel the after-vibration.

Try it.

The first time you tone, whether alone or in a group, you may have difficulty letting go. The inner judge may come to stop you with all sorts of mental chatter to stop you from experiencing your own voice. "Who's listening to me? What do I sound like? My voice sounds strange. This feels weird. This is silly. What does it mean that I'm only toning on one note? Am I doing this right?" If you're in a group you might find yourself comparing your voice to others. Or your voice may be comfortable with low grumbles while everyone else sounds like an angelic choir, and you may judge yourself because you weren't "up there" with everyone else. Remember that everyone is at a different place with their voice, body and emotions. Allow yourself and your voice to be exactly where they are. There is absolutely no right or wrong way to tone. Toning does not have to sound "pretty". Tone again. Notice any changes in your voice and the way you feel. Tone a third time. Each toning is unique. It is a very efficient tune-up.

Toning is the one of the best ways I know to voice emotions, to clear the brain from its constant chatter, to relax, and to bring more energy to the body. After toning students often say they feel clearer, calmer, more in touch with themselves and the group, and more centered emotionally. It is the best way I know to find out more about your voice and its possibilities.

Toning is before technique. It connects us to the primal source of sound, the ancient well which lives inside of each person. Toning is a spontaneous expression of our life force. We can pull sound up from roots of our lives: our hopes, fears, frustrations, sorrows and joys. We mix these with breath. Toning transforms emotions into radiant tones. It can help us to restore our voices and restore our lives. It is not a cure but a means to bring wholeness. Many cultures know this. Our culture is just beginning to rediscover that this type of singing can be a simple but profound way of voicing the soul.

Welcome to the Song Journey.

Opening quote: Joachim-Ernst Berendt, *Nada Brahma The World Is Sound: Music and the Landscape of Consciousness*, Destiny Books, Rochester, Vermont, 1987, p. 171.

1. Joan Halifax, *Shamanic Voices*, E.P. Dutton, New York, 1979, p. 32.
2. Reynold Bean, *unpublished poem*, Albuquerque, New Mexico, 1993.
3. Bernice Johnson Reagon and Sweet Honey in the Rock, *We Who Believe in Freedom: Sweet Honey in the Rock...Still on the Journey;* Anchor Books, New York, 1993, p. 15.

SILENCE

"I sing to thee, Blessed one, with my voice,
and I also sing to thee, Blessed one, through my silence;
for all that my intellect sings with its voice
thou hearest also in its silence."
SYNESIUS OF CYRENE (370~413 AD)

The journey begins with silence.

If the world was created by sound, then what was before sound? Before Sky Woman gave birth to the Tree of Light, she paused in stillness, with no thought, in silence.[1] In Genesis, before God spoke, there was the darkness of the void, the silence of the deep. Before form, before thought, before sound, before creation— is Silence. "The opposite of light is darkness. But the opposite of sound is not silence, which is an intensification of sound. Poets speak of the roaring of silence, of silence as an organ. 'Nothing in the universe'— says Meister Eckhart, 'is so like God as silence.' Silence is wrongly viewed if it is felt to be the opposite of sound. The opposite of sound is noise. Anyone who does not want to listen must at least hear noise."[2]

What is noise in your life? What is silence? Do you spend time with silence each day? Listen to silence with a sleeping cat, a saguaro cactus in the Sonoran Desert, the full moon rising behind a mountain—listen to the mountain. Listen to the silence of space where there are no cash registers, no automobiles, no radios; listen between your inhalation and your exhalation, to the silence between thoughts, to the silence between words. Though everything is made up of vibration, everything contains space and silence as well— space between stars, space between the nucleus of a cell and the cell membrane, the space between strands of DNA. Between each heartbeat is silence.

"Listening is understanding the mystery of vibration beeause listening has to do with inner vibration of the descending intelligence of the moment. Meditators become silence so that they can go to true vibration, which becomes the audible workings of vibration, of which ideas are made."[3]

Before we sing, we must first become receptive to the source of song . Listening becomes the bridge between silence and song: becoming quiet, going within, breathing, listening, deepening into silence, listening for what wishes to be voiced.

All song arises out of this empty place, which is an emptiness full of what nourishes true song— the source of all sounds, out of which all things are created. Listening to the silence brings forth the radiance of song. The presence of silence enters with the breath. On breath, song gives radiance to its origins. To allow the breath of life to move through one's being, one's cell structure, awakens new possibilities of engaging each moment. To sing is to become an instrument of these moments. As we take time to listen, we can begin to find our own unique sound, our own unique response— the voice of our own soul.

Silence

"The mandatory practice of silence and inner emptiness creates a reservoir of intuition for the contemplative musician that defies words. Hildegard of Bingen suggests that 'hearing is receiving' and as such the reception of some rare experiences (one hears both sounds and souls) can cause the hardness of your heart to be shattered. When that kind of hearing has penetrated your center with a seemingly luminous wound, the place where you've been pierced can only be filled with an entirely new kind of love. This new radiance must be returned and sung continuously, or you burn. This burning is a kind of grace, and is the kind of singing that annoints."[4]

Opening quote: Synesius of Cyrene, quoted in Joscelyn Godwin's *Music, Mysticism and Magic: A Sourcebook,* Arkana, New York and London, 1986, p. 31.

1. Paula Gunn Allen, *Grandmothers of the Light: A Medicine Woman's Sourcebook*, Beacon Press, Boston, 1991, p. 44.
2. Joachim-Ernst Berendt, *The Third Ear: On Listening to the World,* Element Books, Longmead, Shaftesbury, Dorset, 1988, p. 72-73.
3. Joseph Rael with Mary Elizabeth Marlow, *Being and Vibration*, Council Oaks Books, Tulsa, 1993, p. 67.
4. Therese Schroeder-Sheker, "Musical-Sacramental-Midwifery: The Use of Music in Death and Dying," Don Campbell (ed.), from *Music and Miracles*, Quest Books, Wheaton, Illinois, 1992, p. 22.

Verse I

Ancient Voices

"Humming and singing, she shaped them. Humming and singing, she placed them where they belonged. That was how the directions came into being. How the seasons came to be."
Paula Gunn Allen

The Keres people believe the world began with Spider Woman singing. Humming and singing she shaped the world. Everything that *is* came from Spider Woman's song.[1]

According to the Athabascan people of Western Canada, the world began when Asintmah wove songs into the Great Blanket of Earth. Everything that *is* began when this first woman sang.[2]

Ancient Egyptian culture believed the world began when the singing sun sang its cry of light. Everything that *is* was brought forth from the singing sun.[3]

For the Aborigines of Australia life began in the Dreamtime when the world was sung into existence. Everything that *is* came from the song of the Dreamtime.[4]

In the Bible the world was created when the Spirit of God moved across the face of the waters and said "Let there be Light!"

And there was light and the world was created. Everything that *is* was brought forth from the sound of God.[5]

Everything begins with song. Earth, ocean, mountain, river, forest, whale, mackeral, buffalo, woman, man, rabbit, hawk, chickadee, rose, grasshopper, spider, corn, beans, peach, plankton, cell, atom. Everything is created from the singing breath of the mythic beings, the gods and goddesses in all cultures of the world. What song does the sperm sound when it enters the egg?

Singing is thought to be the oldest art. Before we could speak, we sang, perhaps not in the way we think of singing today, but a communication through sounds and tones. The evidence is literally in our bones.

"There is anthropological evidence that music came before speech. Ligaments that attach muscles to bones leave traces on the skeletal frame which tell us much about how those muscles were used and make possible reconstructions of the prehistoric creatures from scanty evidence. Our vocal mechanism is complex—for chanting, the lungs and vocal cords are enough; when we speak, the mouth and tongue are drawn into play. Early human skeletal remains reveal signs that the use of the voice to produce speech goes back some eighty thousand years while also suggesting that chanting began perhaps half a million years earlier."[6]

All around the world people sing. The Tohono O'odham people of southern Arizona sing to bring rain to the dry desert. They sing to the feathery red spider, to the sky, to the corn. They pull down the clouds with their song.[7]

People sing. The Eskimo people of eastern Greenland resolve their disputes by singing. They enter the tribal circle armed only with a drum and vent their anger at their opponent through song.[8]

Ancient Voices

All around the world people sing. Kaluli women of New Guinea weep songs when they suffer the loss of a loved one. Grief and remembrance are contained in song.[9]

Apache people sing songs for a young girl's initiation into womanhood. The songs are sung through the life cycles of being a woman as she grows from maidenhood to motherhood. They lead a girl through a beautiful life with their songs.[10]

The people of Classical Greece sang and chanted in the healing temples as they attended the sick. Song was administered along with medicine.[11]

All around the world people sing. Hopis sing up the sun at dawn; Ogalala Sioux create prayers in the sweat lodge; Hawaiians record oral history in chants; every morning Islamic *muezzin* cry prayers to Allah from atop mosque minarets; in the Philippines farmers work and sing as they harvest rice; African fishermen sing while pulling in their nets; merchants in India sing their wares; Buddhist monks recite sutras; we can follow singing everywhere from household to street to continent.

In another time singing was not separate from life, when voices were raised in song over harvested grain... a time when infants were presented to the sun with song... a time when families sang together... a time when *keeners* cried at funerals to open the doorways of grief and everyone would wail and sing at the passing beyond of a loved one... a time when song was used to heal... a time when the earth was blessed with song— on the land, in the lane, in the village, in the plaza, in the home... a time when all the world sang.

How did we become singers? How was the first song created? For what purpose was it created? What did the first songs sound like? We don't know. Our jaw bones are the only artifacts left behind as clues. We can only wonder, and realize this inherent tradition.

I believe singing evolved from the sense of discovery in ancient people, a sense of mystery and engagement with the natural forces that surrounded them— and a need to express this.

Imagine the earth as it was long ago when the first humans emerged: vast open ground, tree-covered hills, mountains, streams, rivers, lakes, ocean, the sun radiant in the sky. Imagine humans before agriculture, villages, cities. Think of early hunter-gatherers living in natural shelters— nomadic... humans before writing, before language as we know it... early humans scattered in small groups throughout the earth. These were the first singers.

Can you imagine how the earth must have sounded then? Can you imagine the sounds of stars singing at night... the sound of a full moon rising over a mountain... the music of the world awakening at dawn... the sounds of a forest at dusk? Can you hear with new ears how it may have been long ago? How could humans not answer back with song?

Imagine wandering into caves glistening with stalactites and stalagmites, like open mouths. Perhaps the first songs were sung here in wonder at the mystery inside the earth, with sounds of awe echoing in the cave's resonant chamber. Imagine that you wandered past meadows in search of food and spied a high mountain range for the first time. Perhaps you could hear the mountains singing to one another— low drones vibrating across the horizon. What songs would mountains inspire?

One could hear rivers, streams, lakes, waterfalls and the different voices of water. How could one not begin to sing with water? Perhaps people sang of gratitude for the life water brings. Water songs would be different from mountain songs. Mountain songs would be different from cave songs. And songs of the sun, lightning and fire would be different than songs of wood. Each tree, each species of tree would have its own song. How could one not join in the chorus of trees? Perhaps your very survival depended upon knowing the songs of the land.

Imagine the sounds of birds and animals at that time: sounds of hunger... sounds of the hunt. Did the first song rise up with the cry of a dying animal— in sympathy with its spirit?

Maybe early peoples sang at night around campfires, huddled together for warmth against the dangers of the night. Perhaps the songs rose up out of small circles of humans sharing the mystery of fire.

Or did song grow from women, mothers in childbirth, mothers comforting babies: soft hums in the early morning when it was still dark and the moon was a cradle in the sky?

Who sang the first song? Greek mythology gives us Orpheus, Dionysus and Pan. The Hopis give us Kokopelli, the hump-backed flute player who brings fertility to the earth and its people. And yet these stories of ancient singers and wandering musicians are relatively recent if song predates speech by hundreds of thousands of years.

Aboriginal creation myths are some of the very oldest stories in existence, perhaps 150,000 years. "All peoples of the world came from us," says an Aboriginal elder. "We have been here before time began. We have come directly out of the Dreamtime of the Creative Ancestors." They tell of "the legendary totemic beings who had wandered over the continent in the Dreamtime singing out the name of everything that crossed their path— birds, animals, plants, rocks, waterholes— and so sang the world into existence."[12]

Perhaps these first songs were born from the rhythm of walking, the syncopation of feet upon the earth— singing the world as a means to bond with the Ancestors. For Aborigines, song exists as a map that helps them find the way through their surroundings. Singing the land is a way to know every step, connect with the stories of the Dreamtime and remember one's place within the web of "continual exchanges." [13]

"The song was supposed to lie over the ground in an unbroken chain of couplets. A couplet for each pair of Ancestor's footfalls, each formed the names they 'threw out' while walking." [14] Singing was a means to name the world and know its form. The trails were referred to as "songlines" and they guided the mythic and ritual structures of community. "The Songlines comprise chapters of a Dreamtime 'Book' of songs, dances and stories. Each story tells about the formation of a place and each place tells a story through its topography and subtle energy." [15] As migratory hunter-gatherers, to integrate with the land is essential for survival. To sing one's environment is to know it deeply, to impress the folds of the land into the folds of the brain.

"I know this may sound far-fetched," says Bruce Chatwin, author of THE SONGLINES, "but if I were asked 'What is the big brain for?' I would be tempted to say 'For singing through the wilderness'." [16] This seems to be another way of saying if you know the song, you can't get lost.

Ancient Egyptians described the tongue as a rudder helping humans steer a course through the world. In another tradition equally old, the tribes of our Northwest Coast sang songs to pass across the waters to far-away places. Certain women sang as navigators. "All she had to know was the song and she knew where she was. To get back, she just sang the song in reverse." [17]

Ancient Voices

Different versions of how the first song arose live throughout the world. Perhaps each legend came from a similar purpose, others may have been created according to unique cultural events. But early stories about singing tell us that one necessity was a connection with the world— and a way to navigate through it like bats sending out sonar to fly through caves.

As I ponder our early beginnings as singers, I am drawn to Bruce Chatwin's vision of "songlines stretching across the continents and ages; that wherever men have trodden they have left a trail of song (of which we may now and then, catch an echo); and that these trails must reach back in time and space, to an isolated pocket in the African savannah, where the First Man opening his mouth in defiance of the terrors that surrounded him, shouted the opening stanza of the World Song, I AM!"[18]

Opening quote: Paula Gunn Allen, *Grandmothers of the Light: A Medicine Woman's Sourcebook,* Beacon Press, Boston, 1991, p. 35.

1. Ibid., pp. 33-37.
2. Merlin Stone, *Ancient Mirrors of Womanhood: Our Goddess and Heroine Heritage,* Volume II, New Sibylline Books, New York, 1979, pp. 97-98.
3. Joachim-Ernst Berendt, *Nada Brahma The World is Sound: Music and the Landscape of Consciousness,* Destiny Books, Rochester, Vermont, 1987, p. 174.
4. Robert Lawlor, *Voices of the First Day: Awakenings in Aboriginal Dreamtime,* Inner Traditions, Rochester, Vermont, 1991, p. 36.
5. Genesis (Chapter 1, Verse 3), *The Bible, King James Version,* World Publishing Co., Cleveland and New York.
6. Yehudi Menuhin and Curtis W.N. Davis, *The Music of Man,* Simon and Schuster, New York, 1979, p. 7.
7. Ruth Murray Underhill, *Singing for Power: The Song Magic of the Papago Indians of Southern Arizona,* University of California Press, Berkeley, California, 1938, pp. 3-4.

8. Edmund Carpenter, *I Breathe a New Song: Poems of the Eskimo,* edited by Richard Lewis, Simon and Schuster, New York, 1971, p. 22.
9. Steven Feld, *Sound and Sentiment: Birds, Weeping, Poetics and Song in Kaluli Expression,* University of Pennsylvania Press, Philadelphia, 1982, p. 33.
10. Penelope Washburn (ed.), *Seasons of Woman: Song, Poetry, Ritual, Prayer, Myth, Story,* Harper and Row, San Francsico, 1979, p. 15.
11. Randall McClellan, *The Healing Force of Music: History, Theory and Practice,* Amity House, Amity, New York, 1988, p. 5.
12. Bruce Chatwin, *The Songlines,* Penguin Books, New York, 1987, p. 2.
13. Gary Snyder, "Poetry and the Primitive: Notes on Poetry as an Ecological Survival Technique", *Earth Household*, New Directions, New York, 1968, p. 129.
14. Chatwin, *The Songlines*, p. 14.
15. Robert Lawlor, *Voices of the First Day: Awakenings in Aboriginal Dreamtime,* Inner Traditions, Rochester, Vermont, 1991, p. 27.
16. Chatwin, *The Songlines,* p. 251.
17. Ibid., p. 283.
18. Ibid., p. 282.

First Voices

"Oh, golden flower opened up
she is our mother
whose thighs are holy
whose face is a dark mask.
She comes from Taoanchan
the first place
where all descended
where all were born."

Poem to the Mother of the Gods (nahuatl)

Our song journey begins before birth when as fetuses curled up in an unfolding spiral, our bodies begin to take form. Throat tissue begins to be formed first out of a matrix that includes genital tissue. Slowly, as we unwind the two tissues begin to take on different functions. The sexual center and the throat center are the creative centers in the body.

Hearing develops in the 4th to 5th month *in utero*. We hear the constant rhythm of our mother's heartbeat. We hear her voice and her inflections. We hear our father's voice and his inflections. We hear the sounds of our home and our world from within the womb. Songs and lullabies should begin before a baby is born.[1] At birth we remember and recognize the voices of our father and mother.

At birth we take our first breath and assert our individuality in the world by making our first cry, singing a distinctive, personal noise. Perhaps our own sounds replace the loss of sounds within our mother's womb, her heartbeat and her breath. We breathe and exchange air with our world and we proclaim how it feels to be in this new world of air after being in the warm liquid of the womb.

In many cultures, people often celebrate this dangerous passage of birth throughout its different phases. During pregnancy, labor, birth, and infancy songs are sung to insure the health and safety of both mother and child.

"There came to me assistance, Mary fair and Bride; as Anna bore Mary, as Mary bore Christ, as Eile bore John the Baptist without flaw in him, aid thou me in mine unbearing, aid me, O Bride!" sing women in Gaelic countries to St. Bridgit or Bride.[2]

In Finland women chant to ease labor pains by summoning the nature spirits. "Pain Spirit, mistress of pain, come here with swift-moving shoes, flutter along in fine skirts; go proudly in black stockings, walk with white stockings to seize fast the pains."[3]

In India songs are sung at the time of delivery. "My life was filled with joy, blessed be my wife's body though her loins were undone with pain."[4]

Mothers are supported by these songs. Old customs welcome babies into the world. Imagine if you had been sung into the world. In contemporary America how many mothers are attended by a chorus of friends? Do doctors and midwives ever sing the child into the world? How many hospitals teach sound and song to the doctors and nurses of their delivery staff? How many doctors or midwives encourage the mother to make her own sounds when she is in labor? Are there any sound coaches present at the birth who will sound in support of the mother's pain?

In the Sumerian myth of Inanna, small helpers mirror the birth pangs of Ereshkigal. She is so grateful she gives them anything they ask for. They ask for Inanna who has been hung on a peg in the underworld by Ereshkigal. Inanna is able to return to life through her sister's gratefulness at having her labor pains sounded and supported by the two helpers. Where are such helpers today?

Leah Maggie Garfield tells a beautiful story in her book Sound Medicine. As she assisted with a birth, she heard what sounded like a little whalesong through the fetal stethoscope. She had never heard anything quite like this before and asked her assistant to listen. They were both puzzled. When the time of birth drew near friends of the mother gathered to sing a welcome song for the newborn. They were delighted and surprised when the baby began to sing with them. He sang the sounds of his whalesong. Garfield believes the song that the baby sang is his *lifesong*— a unique song which exists to guide us through life.[5] Do you know your lifesong?

We each have our own unique vibration, a sound signature that is as individual as our fingerprints. "It is said in the Heikhaloth, the Jewish book of the heavenly spheres, that each time a new soul descends in the ocean of the manifested realm, it generates a vibration which is communicated to the entire cosmic ocean."[6]

In one of my classes a pregnant woman joined us during the last three months of her pregnancy. Often she came with headaches or swollen hands and left feeling better. And though all the women in class were not present at her birth, we did support her in a ritual. I made a small deerskin pouch for the baby and asked each woman to bless a tiny symbolic object and place it inside the pouch. We passed the pouch around the circle and each of us toned into it. We made up the following story:

Now that the light is the light of the summer moon growing to fullness, let the story come and be blown into the pouch...

Once, growing within the pouch of his mother lived an old soul. This soul was as bright as the summer moon, as soft and tender as white deerskin. This soul was unique. Just as you and I have something special, something that only we can bring to the world, this soul also had special gifts to bring. This soul knew stories from ancient times, knew how to fly on wings of imagination, knew how to look into the eyes of another and see the stories which lived there. This soul knew the old tales from a lifetime that he had lived before. This soul brought gifts from that time. . .

This soul comes at this time to bring gifts to his father and mother, light and imagination, courage, wisdom, far-seeing. This soul has walked upon the earth many times, ancient times. This soul is the singer of wisdom, bringer of joy, the one who knew all the stories, ... the one who kept the heart. This soul feels like a heart ...

Oh little one sweet, oh little one mild. I have seen you rest on my feathered wing. We have gone over many canyons together, looked out to those below. It is time to come to this earth plane and bring what you bring to light... I see a soul-baby bringing joy. I see this baby receiving a lot of love. I see this baby being happy to be just the one he is, loved for the one he is. He comes down to this earth from a high place. My prayer is that he will remember when he grows up where he came from . . .

. . . May this child know his own story. May this child know the strength of focusing and the strength of sharing. May this child know he is human and that he is beyond the definition of male and female. May this child feel a part of this world and all he has been. May this child know how unique he is . . .

. . . This young soul/old soul sat in his mother's pouch and listened to the circle of women as they blew their stories, songs and prayers into the pouch. He knew he would remember his pouchful of stories, not all at once. Some he would remember when he was two. Some at four. Some he would tell at eight. Some at eleven. Some stories he would remember at fourteen. Some as a young man. Some as an old man. Just as our stories take time to unfold this soul's stories would unfold out of his life.

. . . I am almost ready. I need just a little more time within your pouch, mother, before I am ready for the world. I am growing strong. When I come out, look into my eyes. Then you will understand the first story I have to tell you.

Little Waysinger, we welcome you!
(The baby was born within the next few days.)

All over the world infants are presented to their communities with song. In the Pueblos of New Mexico along the Rio Grande river a song is sung by the one who first takes the baby from its mother. "Newborn, on the naked sand, nakedly lay it. Next to the earth mother, that it may know her; having good thoughts of her, the food giver."[7]

Jicarilla Apaches of New Mexico sing from sunrise to noon to a newborn four days after birth to ask for supernatural protection of the child. "He sings for long life for the child. He sings of those four rivers, because those rivers have long life, and we people live by means of water."[8]

In East Africa songs accompany naming ceremonies. "And when they name you great warrior, then will my eyes be wet with remembering."[9]

Within our cells we remember these first moments and days of life. We remember in our bodies how we were greeted into the world. Song carries with it a powerful vibration that contains our intentions and our feelings. How different might we all be if we were sung to during birth, during our first few days of life, during our entry into our communities. And since our names carry vibrational patterns, honoring the moment of naming in sacred song would give lifelong blessing to the child.

I was asked to lead a naming ceremony for a baby in Arizona. As family and friends of the child gathered by a pond in a park I welcomed them. I began by saying: "Names are a reflection of our essence, they are chosen with care by our parents. We carry our names with us throughout our lives. During this ceremony allow yourselves to have a sense of wonder. Perhaps you will be doing something for the first time or something you haven't done in a long time. Be like this young babe who has a sense of wonder in discovering the world. During the first part of the ceremony you will be witnesses. Towards the end you will be asked to participate by giving your wishes in song and words."

After a prayer, and a presentation of a flower from the Desert Botanical Garden, the parents recited the history of the name they had chosen for their son and in this way honored their parents and grandparents. They honored a friend by formally naming her as Godmother. We then sang the baby's name three times on a major chord. "When we sing the name lift up your hands imagining we are lifting this child up to the sky. When you bring your voice and hands down imagine bringing your wishes for this child down to earth." I then passed a string and a bowl of blue beads, asking each person to string a bead and speak their special wishes for the baby. We ended by singing *"Somewhere Over the Rainbow."*

As babies, our first language is a form of song. Our first sounds, no matter what culture we are born into, are the sounds "mmmm, mem, mum, mu, me."[10] Already we pay tribute to the muse, to the mother realm, to the ancient ones through these cries.

Baby and mother speak the language of Motherese, a high-pitched sing-song that is mirrored between mother and child. Watch an adult pick up a baby and very shortly you will hear the singing language of Motherese. During the first two years of life babbling, humming, crying, laughing and singing form our response to the world as we communicate our pain and delight. By echoing this back, mothers reassure children that they are being heard and that they are safe. Mothers lull children to sleep with lullabies or humming. "Humming and singing, she shaped them. Humming and singing, she placed them where they belonged."[11] We, too, are shaped by our mother's sounds as she hums and sings to us.

Lullabyes work magic. They touch and surround the child with love and comfort. Pat Carfra, known as the Lullaby Lady, states in a newspaper interview that "the only people who sing to us are the people who love us. When you sing to a child you're reinforcing that."[12] How many of us would be different today if we were lovingly sung to as children? During interviews with over 100 people I asked the question, "were you sung to as a child?" Over half said no. Many couldn't remember whether they were sung to or not. Many said, "not very often."

Those who were sung to as children remember loving the intimacy which lullabyes bring. They felt special as children because they knew that "the songs were just for me." Lullabyes can take away what hurts and replace it with comfort. Many said that being sung to as children made them want to sing. For some it was a normal part of life.

From these early experiences we learn about the magic world singing can create. We are touched inwardly by the voices of our parents or grandparents and feel nurtured. Even off-key singers are appreciated by babies and children because love and warmth are felt through the song. It doesn't matter if the notes aren't quite right. It really doesn't even matter what you sing. What matters is the love.

I was given love through my mother's lullabies and my body knows and remembers the safety and soothing magic she wove through her voice. There have been many times as a music therapist when I have remembered this and sung to my clients. Familiar lullabies, humming or made-up lullabies are used in response to clients in pain. I have used lullabies as a way to bring a client nurturing and centering energy during times of exhaustion, fear, or emotional distress.

When painful childhood memories spontaneously surface and a client needs comforting I sing his or her name on a descending minor third. Universally this is the first interval children sing, it is an archetype of childhood.

When I sing a client's name in this way the response has been consistently positive. Clients report feeling cradled in soothing warmth. Many have said it is the first time they felt safe. One woman said, "it goes straight to my heart." All have told me no one had ever sung their name to them before.

First Voices

Being sung to can bring a sense of safety. This was the case with one of my groups. On Wednesday afternoons, I led a music therapy group with men who were homeless and struggling for recovery from drugs and alcohol, from years of abuse, from years of living on the street, from years of imprisonment, from years of denial, from years of numbing themselves daily with glue, beer, whiskey, cocaine, heroin, cough syrup, anything that would take them away from despair, memories, feelings. I asked them to tell me an image of a safe place. They all answered with images of being alone outdoors— on a mountain; by a stream; in a meadow. Everyone stretched out on the floor and closed their eyes. I mirrored back images of nature in a relaxation and then said "into this safe place allow the song to be with you, let it take you wherever you need to go ..." I sang lullabies, starting out by humming and gradually giving full voice to *"Somewhere Over the Rainbow", "Dear One", "Kentucky Babe", "Autumn to May", "Puff the Magic Dragon"*, and other lullabies that became part of the flow. At first I expected some of them to snicker or open their eyes and scowl at me. Watching the group I noticed their bodies relax a little deeper, faces softening. When I brought them out of the relaxation I asked them to reconnect once again with their safe place. In this section of Albuquerque filled with harsh realities, these men quietly sat up and spoke. "This is the most relaxed I've been." "I've never been sung to before." "It was soothing." "It felt wonderful to have someone sing while I rested."

The human voice has the power to touch others, to give comfort, to provide a feeling of safety. While these men must continue to struggle with recovery, in the safe place of song a moment of childhood became present.

Take a moment in silence. Is there a lullabye you'd like to sing?

Opening quote: Penelope Washbourn (ed.), *Seasons of Woman: Song, Poetry, Ritual, Prayer, Myth, Story,* New York, Harper and Row, 1979, p. 78.

1. Dr. Leon Thurman and Anna Peter Langness, *Heartsong: A Guide to Active Pre-Birth and Infant Parenting through Language and Singing*, Music Study Services, Englewood, Colorado, 1986, p. 6.
2. Penelope Washbourn (ed.), *Seasons of Woman: Song, Poetry, Ritual, Prayer, Myth, Story,* New York, Harper and Row, 1979, p. 95.
3. Ibid., p. 99.
4. David Meltzer (ed.), *Birth: An Anthology of Ancient Texts, Songs, Prayers and Stories,* San Francisco, North Point Press, 1981, pp. 173–174.
5. Leah Maggie Garfield, *Sound Medicine: Healing with Music, Voice and Song,* Berkeley, California, Celestial Arts, 1987, p. 52.
6. Vilayat Inayat Khan, quoted in Joachim-Ernst Berendt, *Nada Brahma The World is Sound: Music and the Landscape of Consciousness,* Rochester, Vermont, Destiny Books, 1987, p. 34.
7. Penelope Washbourn (ed.), *Seasons of Woman: Song, Poetry, Ritual, Prayer, Myth, Story,* New York, Harper and Row, 1979, p. 104.
8. David Meltzer (ed.), *Birth: An Anthology of Ancient Texts, Songs, Prayers and Stories,* San Francisco, North Point Press, 1981, pp. 173–174.
9. Ibid., p. 215.
10. Nor Hall, *The Moon and the Virgin*, Harper and Row, New York, 1980, p. 28.
11. Paula Gunn Allen, *Grandmothers of the Light: A Medicine Woman's Sourcebook,* Beacon Press, Boston, 1991, p. 35.
12. Pat Carfra, The Globe and Mail, Newspaper interview, October 28, 1987.

Childhood Voices

"Sing a song of sixpence,
A pocketful of rye;
Four and twenty blackbirds
Baked in a pie.
When the pie was opened,
The birds began to sing;
Was that not a dainty dish
To set before the king?"
Traditional Nursery Rhyme

All over the world, between the 12th and 15th month of life, children sing their first interval, the descending minor third. You know it. It is the first two notes of *"Rain Rain Go Away"*, the first two notes of "It's raining, it's pouring, the old man is snoring . . .", the first two notes of "nyah nyah nyah nyah nyah . . ."

All around the world children sing. Between ages two and three children begin to sing and remember nursery rhymes and simple songs on their own. During this time they spontaneously make up songs about their world and how they feel. Children go back and forth between singing and speaking.[1] They make up to as many as ten songs per hour. When they get ready to go outside to play they might make up a song about putting on shoes. As they play outside they may get interested in a stick and start waving it in the air, making up a song as they move. Making up songs is an inclination as natural as breathing and as natural as our heartbeat. Songs inhabit the air every moment around the world.

As children hear other people singing, their spontaneous songs may contain fragments of the songs that they hear. Bits of "*Twinkle Twinkle Little Star*" may be interspersed with humming or scales or songs about the wind. Somewhere around age four "the learned song assumes dominance over the spontaneous song."[2]

As children learn more words the musical sounds in their speech begin to fall away. They may begin to feel a pressure to sound more like grown-ups. "By the time children are four or five years old, many have taken in negative messages about their natural expressive musical selves. 'Stop whining', 'Don't talk like a baby', 'Say it like a grown-up' are all common messages children hear about their growing facilities with speech. From this, they frequently perceive that there is something wrong with their natural spontaneous expression."[3]

Our voice is first felt inside of us, so when someone criticizes our voice we often feel criticized as people. Such messages have the power to take our voices away:

• A woman remembers Catholic grade school. After listening to all of the children sing, the Nuns separated them into two groups. One group was pinned with blue paper dots. The other group had white paper dots pinned to their dresses or shirts. The blue dots were the singers. Those with white dots were relegated to be listeners. They could listen to the singers.

Childhood Voices

Once during a school performance the blue dots sang *"How Much Is That Doggy In The Window?"* The white dots were allowed to bark at a certain place in the song. This woman vividly remembers being branded a *non-singer* in childhood. She never sang again in front of people. "The only time I ever sang after that was to my children when they were babies and I sang to put them to sleep." Even though her husband's family all get together on the front porch and sing along with guitars, she listens. Everyone else sings. She listens.

• "There are singing birds and there are listening birds", another woman remembers a teacher saying. She, of course, was a listening bird. I have also heard the same story with these changes: "there are singing birds and there are black birds." The *non-singers* are the black birds. In one classroom the children were asked to sing a song into a tape recorder to make a group tape as a Christmas present for their parents. One woman remembers being asked to recite a poem instead. Being told to sit at the back of the choir or to "mouth the words" are also common stories of early singing experiences in school or church. In a questionnaire with over 100 respondents over half were told to stop singing by a teacher, parent or sibling. Many stopped singing for years or never again sang in front of another person. If they sang they became secret singers.

When asked how it made them feel to be told to stop singing, people told me they were hurt and felt angry, rejected, embarrassed, and worthless. For some it was yet another failure. Many said it made them quit singing.

Many times children are asked to stop singing because they are "out of tune". While there are some people who are tone deaf, many children labeled out of tune are simply inexperienced in listening to music. Many people have come to my classes over the years who insist that they are tone deaf. When I listen carefully to them I find that they are not out of tune, just very shy and insecure about their voices. They carry negative labels as if branded with them. And even when someone seems truly out of tune their voices can usually be helped with time, patience, and encouragement. Should people who can't carry a tune be denied their human right to sing? Perhaps some people won't fit into a choir where precision and harmony are important, but many other ways exist to enjoy and benefit from singing and expressing oneself through sound. When an over-emphasis on technique begins too early in school many people stop singing. Unless we are going to make a living with our voices, why should it matter if our voice isn't polished or is off-key once in a while?

Singing brings a sense of community and allows a child to feel part of a greater harmony. When children are encouraged they sing and enjoy themselves. As a child I remember making up songs and singing on the school bus with friends. Most of my favorite memories of childhood revolve around singing. Many people have warm memories of singing in the car with family, Christmas caroling, or singing at camp late at night around the fire.

Singing allows children a means of creative rebellion against the rules and structures of school. Radio personality and author Garrison Keillor remembers "as we marched toward school we'd all sing to ourselves the marching songs of children. We'd sing:

Mine eyes have seen the glory of the burning of the school
We are torturing the teachers we are breaking all the rules
We broke into his office and we tickled the princepool

and truth goes marching on
Glory glory hallelujah
Teacher hit me with a ruler
I bopped her on the bean with a rotten tangerine
And she ain't gonna teach no more."[4]

Singing helps children learn. In San Diego, California teachers write songs to incorporate information from their lesson plans. "By singing the song, students are fixing both facts and the emotions associated with them in long-term memory."[5]

Singing stimulates creative expression in children. Many of the words in children's songs are imaginative and inventive. As I was growing up my love for words became stimulated by songs such as:

"If I Only Had a Brain"
from THE WIZARD OF OZ
"I could while away the hours
Conferrin' with the flowers
Consultin' with the rain
And my head I'd be scratchin'
While my thoughts were busy hatchin'
If I only had a brain."[6]

"Supercalifragilisticexpialidocious"
from MARY POPPINS
"Even though the sound of it is something quite atrocious
If you say it loud enough you're sure to sound precocious
Supercalifragilisticexpialidocious."[7]

"Zip-A-Dee-Doo-Dah"
from SONG OF THE SOUTH
"Zip-A-Dee-Doo-Dah
Zip-A-Dee-A
My oh my what a wonderful day
Plenty of sunshine
Heading my way
Zip-A-Dee-Doo-Dah
Zip-A-Dee-A"[8]

Singing encourages better breathing and posture. (Something that is needed when children sit at uncomfortable school desks concentrating on difficult problems for hours at a time.)

Because much of the wounding that comes to the voice occurs in childhood I often use children's songs in my classes as a way to both bring out these issues and also help to resolve them. Singing children's songs often brings out the playful side of ourselves which is less self-conscious about how we sound. A business executive, depressed over the loss of a job, felt like a different person after he sang a remembered favorite song from childhood:

"I can't get off of my horse
All day I ride with the cattle
I can't get off of my horse
'Cause some dirty dog put glue on my saddle."

Every now and again in the *Joy of Singing* classes profound silliness rises to the surface. Silliness that makes us dance and sing to stuffed animals. Silliness that makes us march around the room to Wizard of Oz tunes. We are inspired to sing gibberish to one another or croon to the moon like Bing Crosby. When such moments arise I know it is time to introduce Clara Cluck.

Clara Cluck was the cartoon chicken of my childhood. Do you remember her? She was an opera singer. She wore a large plumed hat, held her hands in front of her ample chicken bosom and sang high Italian opera with her clucks.

Try it yourself. Stand with chest beaming with the pride of your magnificent chicken voice. Hold your arms in a circular fashion with your hands held together in front of your heart. Take in a deep breath, savoring the high drama of the moment, and cluck out your favorite operatic or classical tune.

Laughter helps free the voice. Or pretend you're Bing Crosby crooning Blue Moon or, my personal favorite, "I'm forever blowing bu-bu-bu-bubbles."

If you might be too embarrassed to try these alone (who knows which neighbor might be looking in the window), then try it next time you're with a small child. Play Clara Cluck or Singing Bing together. Remember a time when you made up songs about mud puddles and rain. Remember a time when you laughed out loud when you played in the snow. Remember a time when your pet dog knew just what you were saying.

Opening quote: Nursery Rhyme, Mabel Williams and Marcia Dalphin, (eds.), Junior Classics Vol. 10, Collier & Son, New York, 1938, p. 3.

1. Hollace Anne Veldhuis, "Spontaneous Song of Pre-School Children", *The Arts In Psychotherapy,* 1984, p. 15.
2. Don G. Campbell, *Introduction to the Musical Brain,* Magnamusic-Baton, Saint Louis, 1984, p. 51.
3. Shelley Katsh and Carole Merle-Fishman, *The Music Within You,* Simon and Schuster, New York, 1985, p. 33.

4. Garrison Keillor, audiotape, "The Seasons, Spring", Minnestoa Public Radio.
5. Stephanie Merritt, *Successful, Non-Stressful Learning: Applying the Lozanov Method to All Subject Areas,* Learning to Learn, San Diego, 1987, p. 132.
6. *"If I Only Had A Brain"*, The Wizard of Oz, Leo Feist, New York, 1968, p. 29.
7. *"Supercalifragilisticexpialidocious"*, from the film Mary Poppins.
8. *"Zip-A-Dee-Doo-Dah"*, from the film Song of the South.

Chorus

Sacred Voices

"We are no longer able to hear the Buddha's voice. However, we can still hear voices that come close to his . When all things of this world that have a voice together raise their voices, retaining their individual character yet combining them in one large sound, then we are very, very close to the sound of the Buddha's voice."
from the SHOJI JISSO-GI

All over the world people use song as a way to praise the Creator. People use song as a way to pray, as a way to reach the Divine. "The Spirit will not descend without song"[1] says an old African proverb. A more contemporary gospel echoes the same thought: "let us sing 'til the power of the Lord comes down."[2]

Song touches the spirit. As we breathe in we become touched by Divine Life. We take air inside and let it mingle with our blood. When we breathe out, that breath becomes a song by which our spirit enters the world to communicate with others.

For the Eskimo, "songs are born in stillness while all endeavored to think of nothing, but of beautiful things. Then they (the songs) take shape in the minds of men and rise up like bubbles from the depths of the sea; bubbles seeking the air in order to burst. This is how the sacred songs are made."[3]

For the Navajo "the most potent force in the universe is wind, given form in speech and song."[4]

In the Jewish Mystical tradition of Kabbalism, angels actually need our songs. "It is believed that those angels who sing by night are the leaders of all other singers. When we terrestrial creatures raise up our hearts in song, then those supernatural beings gain an accession of knowledge, wisdom and understanding. They are able to perceive matters which even they before had never comprehended."[5]

Song begins with breath. To breathe is to be alive. Breath permeates and touches every cell of our bodies. Breath is invisible and mysterious. We share our breath with every living thing. The same air I breathe is used by trees, hummingbirds, eagles, foxes, mountains. People in China, Israel and Brazil all breathe the air I breathe. "Each one of us, with every breath we take, exhales or inhales a few dozen of the same electrons that Julius Caesar expelled with his last sigh at the moment of his assassination in 44 BC . . . a few of these oldest electrons are in each one of us. And each one of us . . . has electrons that have been part of Jesus or the Buddha or other great saints and seers in history, electrons charged with their photon information, their photon cognition, their photon love. In each one of us, on the other hand, are also the electrons that have been in (and are thus programmed by) people like Hitler and Stalin, Himmler and Eichmann."[6]

These electrons enter through our breath. Through breath we are literally linked with every living thing, both present and past. In this fact lies the heart of mystery. The word *breath* in many cultures means Spirit. We are inspired when we breathe, in-filled with Spirit, with the force that moves through the sea, rocks, butterflies, our cells, every living thing.

Perhaps one reason why song has been used in prayer and worship is precisely its connection to breath. We don't see breath, spirit, or song, but we experience all three. "When we study the science of breath the first thing we notice is that breath is audible; it is a word in itself, for what we call a word is only a more pronounced utterance by breath fashioned by the mouth and the tongue. In the mouth breath becomes voice, and thereby the original condition of a word is breath. If we said, 'First was the breath', it would be the same as saying 'In the beginning was the word.' "[7]

Breathing exchanges what is outside to what is inside, and from what is inside to what is outside. We commune with Spirit through our breath and through our song.

Song has been part of spiritual worship as prayer, praise and meditation. We pray for many reasons. Many times I pray because I feel cut off from a spiritual source and long to connect with something greater than myself. When my prayers are most effective they involve emotion-fueled song and not just words. My prayer opens up as a cry to God. Other people throughout the world also use prayer in this way. "When the Israelites were held captive in Egypt, it was their groaning that touched God in a special way. The psalmist and the prophets prayed with groans and sighs, especially during times of intense shame, grief, sorrow, misery and oppression. For thousands of years, until this day, the Jewish people have carried on the tradition of lamentation by crying out to God at the wailing wall on the western side of the Temple in Jerusalem."[8]

A minister, who is a friend of mine, calls this kind of prayer "knocking loudly on the door of the Lord." I have had several dramatic experiences through song while "knocking loudly on the door of the Lord." Many years ago my husband and I knew we wanted to move from Albuquerque to a more rural environment outside of the city. We looked for a house for a long time. Finally we found a wonderful old adobe near the river. We gave notice to our landlord and said yes to the adobe. We were making plans to move when we got a call saying the house was already taken. We were devastated and didn't know how we could find a house, especially with the environment we wanted, in less than three weeks. I started to cry. As I cried, I began to wail and tone and pray. Instead of thinking about a house, I kept praying, "Please Lord, all I want is a piece of earth on which I can sit and call home."

I imagined sitting on rocks in a beautiful setting. That night I saw an ad in the paper for a house in the east mountain area outside of Albuquerque. This was a very different area than the north valley where we had been looking. It would mean a drive of at least a half an hour into the city to work. We decided to go and take a look and that night drove out to see this house. We arrived in the dark and couldn't see the land, but imagined the house would have a beautiful setting. The agent wanted an answer immediately, but we needed 24 hours to decide. With little sleep, we drove back up to see the house at dawn. When I saw it I knew we had found our *home*.

The house is perched atop a hill with beautiful views of South Mountain and Sandia Mountain. It is on a dead-end street right next to a 40-acre parcel of national forest. In this forest I have found my place to sit on the rocks surrounded by beauty. When we walk in the forest, we see no one except rabbits, flickers, hummingbirds, squirrels, jays and other wildlife. We've lived here five years now. "I cried unto God with my voice, even unto God with my voice, and he gave ear to me."[9] Prayer fueled by emotion and song is powerful.

There exists another type of emotional prayer— praise of thanksgiving, when we are overflowing with love and gratitude to the Creator. These prayers are like the psalms which urge us to "make a joyful noise unto the Lord, all ye lands. Serve the Lord with gladness, come before his presence with singing."[10]

Joachim-Ernst Berendt tells us that "music was first created as a means of adoration. So as to sing the praise of the gods and God in joy and exaltation."[11] This type of praising through song is called a jubilus or jubilation. The jubilation comes when there is a realization that "words cannot express the inner music of the heart."[12] A jubilation is "the voice of a heart dissolved in joy."[13] Have there been times when love welled up inside of you and you just had to sing?

When we see something beautiful or moving there is a natural human impulse to let out the sound "Ahhhhh." We are in awe of the Creator's magnificent creation and words no longer suffice. In many of the esoteric systems that give tones to the seven chakras, "Ah" is the sound given to the heart. "Ah" is a root sound in the Christian tradition of Amen, Allelujah and Hosanna. Since Christ's message is a message of love, perhaps there would no longer be religious wars if both sides sat down together to sing "Ahhhhhhh."

Another way prayer works is through repetition of a mantra or chant. The repetition acts to let go of the conscious mind in order to achieve a state of oneness. Vilayat Inayat Khan says that "in the mantra practice one actually kneads the very flesh of our body with sound."[14] Mantras act as "tools for becoming one."[15] They contain seed sounds like "Hu" or "Om" which affect us in profound ways.

"The sages of India and Tibet as well as the monks of Sri Lanka feel that if there is a sound audible to us mortals that comes close to the primal sound that is the world, then it is the sound of the sacred word Om."[16]

Repetition works as an important way to make the sound of mantras, prayers or chants an integral part of daily experience. Catholics go into profound states of meditation through using the rosary. East Indians do this through chanting with their mala beads. Pueblo Indians enter into meditative states through ritualized chanting, drumming and dancing. The words, sounds, and steps repeat over and over again until the singers become one with the sounds.

Tibetans have used mantras for centuries. They "are a very practical people. Were they merely the esoteric mystics that they are in the eyes of the Western world, they could never have survived in the harsh mountain world of snow and ice. They would not recite mantras for half a lifetime, had they not tested and experienced again and again the power of such syllables and sounds in themselves."[17]

Song has been part of worship services since the earliest times. Hebrews, Mayans, Aztecs, Bushmen, Muslims, Christians, Buddhists, Sufis, Quakers, Shakers, Eskimos, Catholics, Seneca, Hopi, and most every culture and religion use song as part of their worship. Can you imagine a place of worship without singing? And yet I have heard many of my students say that in their search to find a church they attended several where there was no singing and several where only the choir sang.

Last Easter I went with my husband to Santuario de Chimayo. This small chapel is considered to be a place of healing by the peoples of New Mexico. The dirt inside the chapel contains healing properties. A room off the chapel is filled with crutches, casts, glasses and other objects left there by people who no longer needed them because their prayers had been answered. Throughout Holy Week between Palm Sunday and Easter, hundreds of people walk, sometimes hundreds of miles, from their homes on pilgrimages to this tiny chapel.

On this holy day, in this holy place, I could count on one hand the number of people singing the familiar Easter hymns. The words of the hymns were provided for everyone. One singer's voice blared over the microphone but hardly anyone sang with her. People were spectators— not participants in-spirited through song. How can we know our own souls if we do not sing? How can we share our spiritual feelings with each other?

Hafiz, the great poet of fourteenth century Persia told the following legend:

"God made a statue of clay in His own image, and asked the soul to enter into it, but the soul refused to be imprisoned, for its nature is to fly about freely and not to be limited and bound to any sort of capacity. The soul did not wish in the least to enter this prison. Then God asked the angels to play their music and as the angels played the soul was moved to ecstacy, and in order to make the music more clear to itself, it entered the body." [18]

Hafiz is said to have added: "people say the soul, on hearing that song, entered the body: but in reality the soul itself is song." [19]

Many different ways exist to use song as prayer. Sometimes the most effective prayer is entering into silence. For philosopher Sören Kirkegaard "...praying is hearing, not merely being silent. This is how it is. To pray does not mean to listen to oneself speaking. Prayer involves becoming silent, and being silent, and waiting until God is heard."

Opening quote: "Shoji jisso-gi", Japanese Buddhist text, quoted in Joachim-Ernst Berendt's *Nada Brahma The World Is Sound: Music and the Landscape of Consciousness,* Destiny Books, Rochester, Vermont, 1987, p. 155.

1. LeRoi Jones, *Blues People,* William Morrow and Company, New York, 1963, p. 41.
2. Traditional gospel from Ysaye Barnwell with George Brandon, *Singing in the African American Tradition: Choral and Congregational Vocal Music,* Woodstock, Homespun Tapes, New York, 1989, p. 29.
3. Nor Hall, *The Moon and the Virgin,* Harper and Row, New York, 1980, p. 178.
4. David P. McAllester, "Coyote's Song", in PARABOLA MAGAZINE, *Music, Sound and Silence,* Volume V, Number 2, 1980, pp. 52-53.
5. Joscelyn Godwin, *Harmonies of Heaven and Earth: The Spiritual Dimensions of Music,* Inner Traditions, Rochester, Vermont, 1987, p. 73.
6. Joachim-Ernst Berendt, *Nada Brahma The World Is Sound: Music and The Landscape of Consciousness,* Destiny Books, Rochester, Vermont, 1987, p. 125.
7. Hazrat Inayat Khan, quoted in Joachim-Ernst Berendt's *Nada Brahma The World Is Sound: Music and the Landscape of Consciousness,* Destiny Books, Rochester, Vermont, 1987, p. 33.
8. Steven Halprin with Louis Savary, *Sound Health: The Music and Sounds That Make Us Whole,* Harper and Row, San Francisco, 1985, p. 169.
9. Psalms 77, *The Bible, King James.*
10. Psalms 100, Verses 1 and 2, *The Bible.*
11. Joachim-Ernst Berendt, *The Third Ear: On Listening to the World,* Element Books, Longmead, Shaftesbury, Dorset, 1985, p. 194.
12. R.J. Stewart, *Music and the Elemental Psyche,* Destiny Books, Rochester, Vermont, 1987, p. 144.
13. Robert Maynard, "The Jubilus: A Form of Meditative Chanting", MATRIX, January 1989, p. 20.
14. Joachim-Ernst Berendt, *Nada Brahma The World Is Sound: Music and The Landscape of Consciousness,* Destiny Books, Rochester, Vermont, 1987, p. 41.

15. Ibid., p. 27.
16. Ibid., p. 28.
17. Ibid., p. 41.
18. Hazrat Inayat Khan, *The Music of Life*, New Mexico, Santa Fe, Omega Books, 1983, p. 71.
19. Ibid., p. 71.

Voices of Courage and Hope

We shall overcome
We shall overcome
We shall overcome someday
Oh deep in my heart
I do believe
that we shall overcome someday

"One cannot describe the vitality and emotion this one song evokes across the Southland. I have heard it sung in great mass meetings with a thousand voices singing as one; I've heard a half-dozen sing it softly behind the bars of the Hinds County Prison in Mississippi; I've heard old women singing it on the way to work in Albany, Georgia; I've heard the students singing it as they were dragged away to jail. It generates power that is indescribable."
Wyatt Tee Walker

Song has been used throughout the ages to bring strength, hope and unity during times of oppression and distress. The very act of singing puts us in touch with the sustaining force of life.

Singing helps us draw upon the deep reservoir of our feelings. Rather than collapsing in tears, fears or anger we can use our emotions as fuel for song. This allows our emotions to be expressed and heard. Reaching out through the voice connects us with more than ourselves. We become part of the Great Spirit that permeates all life. This is an empowering experience. Throughout the world, song has been used in this way.

We can draw from slavery and the Civil Rights movement to give us examples of how song has been used to generate hope and power. Imagine being taken from your home, from your family, your people, your country and placed in a strange land where your language, religious beliefs, and customs were not understood or valued. You could no longer practice your beliefs but had to take on the beliefs of others. You could no longer play your music or dance the tribal dance. All these things were forbidden in order to break your spirit.

A device called a "bit" was sometimes used. Similar to a horse's bit, it was used to treat someone like an animal— "to stop you from talking, silence, having no language, not being able to express anything. Imposing this should destroy you. All human qualities should evaporate."[1] This was the experience of slavery.

But when African chants were denied, song still found its way out through Biblical images and became the legacy of spirituals. These songs were sung in the fields, at church, or alone; they gave solace and power to the spirit.

When a plantation owner wouldn't allow slaves to meet "they would take one of the slave cabins and put a big black iron wash pot in the middle of the floor so the sound of the singing would go into the pot and not out the door."[2]

The songs reflected loneliness:
  Sometimes I feel like a motherless child
  Sometimes I feel like a motherless child
  Sometimes I feel like a motherless child
  A long way from home

The songs reflected despair:
  They sold my children away, Lord
  They sold my children away
  I wish I never was born

The songs reflected weariness:
  Soon I will be done with the troubles of the world
  Goin' home to live with God

The songs reflected the triumph of spirit:
  There is trouble all over this world
  But I ain't gonna lay my religion down

The songs reflected political messages:
  Go down Moses
  Way down to Egypt land
  Tell your Pharaoh
  Let my people go

The songs reflected hope:
  There'll be freedom in that land
  There'll be freedom in that land
  There'll be freedom in that land
  Where I'm bound

Reverend Marshall Smith, a gospel singer and pianist with the group *The Golden Voices* since 1957, says that during slavery, "there were things that couldn't be uttered orally so they came out in song. For instance, *'Steal Away, Steal Away, Steal Away to Jesus.'* When they was singing that song it could have also meant that we gonna get away from this as well. You may not be allowed to do or say some things but normally most people don't interfere with you too much when you're talking to Jesus. That was a method of getting the message over. Another traditional spiritual, *'Somebody's Knocking at Your Door'* was used to say we are here now but we're pushing for a better place."

The Old Testament was used as a source for many of the spirituals because of the recurrent theme of repression and deliverance in Old Testament stories: Daniel was delivered from the lion's den; Moses freed the Hebrews from the Egyptians; David triumphed over Goliath. And the white man's Bible said these things were true. The spirituals, grown out of these stories, were powerful songs of hope. If not in this world, then in the next.

During the Civil Rights movement, song was used as a powerful unifying force. I asked Reverend Smith about his experiences of this time: "Singing was an important part of our activities. When Arthurine Lucy was trying to go to Alabama University, I was there when that was going on in Tuscaloosa. Pollyann Myers was expelled because she had been married and divorced. They'll find something to try and stop you. We was taught to not fight back. Do it with kindness. If an egg was thrown on us we would walk and when the mass met, police would come and state troopers would walk through the churches where we was gathered. Martin Luther King and Ralph Abernathy and all of them was there when wc first started. Andrew Young, and all that group of ministers was there, they started right there in Birmingham. When the police would come through we made no noise, we would just sing. They did nothing to us except they would walk through with these billy sticks and go back down the aisle. We would just sing *'We Shall Overcome'* or something of that sort. We would sing *'Oh Freedom'* and *'Before I'll be a slave I'll be buried in my grave and go home and live with Jesus and be saved.'* If we were to get up and start to go out the aisle, even if we was just going to the bathroom, we might have been beaten. Just think what it could have been. We looked at it from the standpoint that it was Satan's spirit moving down the aisle. The only way he could get in is through us. If we rebelled in any way you could've been killed. You would have been badly beaten up. But we was taught to sing and we would sing.

"When we'd get to singing, *'When All God's Children Get Together, What a Time, What a Time'* the police would be trying to stand straight but you'd catch them moving to the beat 'cause there was rhythm and there was something about it that was real. We overcame that through song. Instead of getting up and saying, 'get back, get back,' no one would utter a word. We'd just move back and keep singing.

These were things that were very helpful. Singing soothes. It does something for you and it will calm you in your most weakest hour. You utter a song and you're in a different spirit, a different attitude will come and it will lighten you up, like a rose when it's blooming.

"The singing fills the emptiness that you was feeling. You was feeling a void spirit because you didn't know what was coming up. Songs were utilized as a shield 'cause you know you couldn't resort to warfare. If 35 or 40 of us got up to fight, they'd have 150

National Guard there so you couldn't put up that kind of a fight and you wouldn't want to, anyway. So we sang and that's a shield between you and harm. Most people are not going to harm you if you are singing. They might tell you to shut up and you just hush and stop and then you go right back out and do it again. So they leave you alone. That is a shield.

"I think there would have been much more bloodshed had we not had singing. Very much prayer was put in this. When it comes to singing, everyone could tune in. The song is a prayer you're uttering up in tones. You can't speak what you really want to speak, but if you have the right attitude, that attitude of negativeness will be removed at the deliverance of the song. How can I sit and have a negative attitude towards you if you're singing, *'He's Got the Whole World in His Hands'* when I know that's a fact. We didn't create this world. I think singing was very instrumental in keeping the peace during that time. It's essential for each individual to put in effort. When efforts are put in by both sides we can be victorious. We need to put this in our singing."

When I asked Rev. Smith if he had something to say about song as an ingredient in hope, his eyes lit up as he replied:

"One old number comes to mind: *'We Shall Walk Through the Valley in Peace.'* We do a version of that where we use the setting of the 23rd Psalm, 'The Lord is my Shepherd, I shall not want, all the downtrodden . . .' If you wanna keep yourself there you do that but you can be raised from that because He is your shepherd and you shall not want and if you take that and make it joyous. What comes from the heart is the issues of life and when it flows out you see your story realistically and things happen.

"For instance, this person came and they didn't have no bread and you let them know you've been there. And if you overcame it so can they. When I left home travelling as a gospel pianist we got to Indiana where we was gonna base. I didn't have a dime to call the sponsor and let him know we was there. We had sponsors for a year at a time. They'd contract with us in various parts of Indiana and all around wherever they booked us. I didn't have a dime. But I was determined that I would go. I stepped outside, got off the bus and I was going to go ask someone how to get to such and such an area and then I was going to start walking. But there was a dime right there as I stepped out. That gave me courage. Then I could sing, 'when the storms of life are raging, Lord, stand by me.' And He stood by me because there was a dime that I didn't have laying there for me to call the sponsor.

" The person had an apartment for us to stay in, our bookings starting out within 3 days already for us. I wouldn't have known that if I didn't have the dime to call. I couldn't have gotten there. These things are the things you base your singing on. Sometimes I get to praising God here in my home in Albuquerque. When I left home and got to Indiana I didn't have no cookware. So we bought a can of peaches and cooked our bacon and eggs in that peach can 'cause that's all we had. When we made a little money we went to the Salvation Army and bought a lot of cookware. You could buy things for 10¢ or 15¢. We bought what we needed. I've experienced that.

"I walk into my kitchen now and all back in the garage and we've got every kind of cookware you could want. Now that gives me something to sing about 'cause I had the experience. This gives you a song, 'I've got joy, joy, joy, joy down in my soul. I've got the love of Jesus down in my soul.' You can relate to that 'cause you have been down there and you can rise above it. If you just continue the faith. That's really where songs come from.

"Like the song *'His Eye is on the Sparrow .'* When you think about that little bitty birdie, that little bit of a birdie, and there you are almost a million times bigger than that birdie and you know if He sees that birdie then He watches over you then you can belt that out. 'His eye is on the sparrow and I know He watches me.' It gives you a deeper meaning when you really know what you're singing about."

Rev. Smith did not always think of himself as a singer. He told me, "Your attitude determines your altitude. If you have a bad attitude you ain't gonna get too high. I used to carry the theory that I cannot sing. But not any more. I got past it by sitting down in a silent moment and I began to think. I said to myself, 'now I may not be as good as some of those people who can sing but I can be right in the game. You might be up here but I'm going to be right back here. I may not sound like you but I can do it.' I based that in my mind and upon basing that I became victorious and I got to where I could sing. I got confidence now that I can do it so I get with it. I feel like if I enjoy it then somebody else will. When I get joy out of singing I know I can reach somebody else."

Today, *Sweet Honey in the Rock,* led by founder Bernice Johnson Reagon, keeps alive songs of courage and hope. For twenty years this diverse and ever-changing group of African-American women sing out for freedom all over the world. Writer Alice Walker has attended many *Sweet Honey in the Rock* concerts. She writes, "These songs said— we do not come from people who had nothing. We come rather from people who've had everything — except money, except political power, except freedom. They said: yes, we were captured. They chained our grandmother to the mast of a ship and carried her away from every other face truly reflecting her own; her last view of home being perhaps, that face resembling her own counting the money from her sale. They said: yes, they hanged your Indian grandfather from the tree beneath which he worshipped life. And, yes, the singers said, it is not over yet. For we are still captive! Look at the lies, the evasions, the distortions of truth with which we live our lives."[3]

Singing, when used in this way, liberates— both spiritually and psychologically. One gains confidence to take political action. To have a voice is to take a stand for what one believes. These songs of protest are songs that generate spirit, justice and community. They are songs to wake us up to abuses of racism and persecution. They are not songs of anger but songs of love for social justice, freedom for all peoples of the world.

When two civil rights workers were wrongfully jailed and put in solitary confinement, they were able to hear each other through a small vent in the door. "We sang. As the police pounded on the door, threatening to whip us, we sang, *'Woke Up This Morning With My Mind On Freedom.'* Even after they turned the heaters on and blasted us with unbearable heat for seven days, we continued to sing . . . 'We'll walk hand in hand'."[4] What made the unbearable bearable was singing. And through the song holding onto the belief that *'We Shall Overcome'*.

The spiritual power of *"We Shall Overcome"* remains very much alive. Sung in Germany as the Berlin Wall fell, it was was also sung in China at Tiananmen Square. A universal testament to hope, the song belongs to us all. It is needed today when women are raped and not believed. It is needed today when children are molested and not protected. It is needed today when acid rain kills forests. It is needed today for the AIDS epidemic. It is needed for Gay Rights. Wherever people are oppressed, the song offers a vehicle for the hope to persevere and find justice.

Voices of Courage and Hope

Sing along with the words to help you through your own struggles when you need hope:

We shall overcome
We shall overcome
We shall overcome someday
Oh deep in my heart
I do believe
That we shall overcome someday

2) We are not afraid (3x) today! ...
3) We shall stand together ...
4) The truth will make us free ...
5) The Lord will see us through ...
6) We shall live in peace ...
7) The whole wide world around ...
8) We are not alone ...
9) We'll walk hand in hand ... [5]

Make up your own verses.

Opening quote: *We Shall Overcome: Songs of the Freedom Movement,* compiled by Guy and Candie Carawan for the Student Non-Violent Coordinating Committee, Oak Publications, New York, 1963, p. 11.

1. Toni Morrison, interview with Melvyn Bragg, *The South Bank Show,* London Weekend Television, Oct. 11, 1987.
2. Bernice Johnson Reagon and Sweet Honey in the Rock, *We Who Believe in Freedom; Sweet Honey in the Rock . . . Still on the Journey,* Anchor Books, New York, London, Toronto, Sydney, Auckland, 1994, p. 145.
3. Ibid., p. 9.

4. Guy and Candie Carawan (eds.), *We Shall Overcome: Songs of the Freedom Movement*, Oak Publications, New York, 1963, p. 90.
5. Peter Blood-Patterson (ed.), *Rise Up Singing*, Sing Out Corporation, Bethlehem, Pennsylvania: 1988, p. 63.

Healing Voices

"What kind of music can heal?... Singing is the most powerful, for singing is living. It is Prana. The voice is life itself."
Sufi Inayat Khan

In the beginning of Women Who run with the Wolves, Clarissa Pinkola Estes tells the story of a woman named La Loba who collects wolf bones from dry riverbeds, from mountains, from the fine-sifted earth of the desert. When she has gathered all of the bones she puts them together, until the entire skeleton of the wolf is before her. She stands and sings over the bones until a wolf is fleshed out by the power of her song. As the wolf is freed, it runs through the desert and turns into a laughing woman running free.

"In the tale, La Loba sings over the bones she has gathered. To sing means to use the soul-voice. It means to say on the breath the truth of one's power and one's need, to breathe soul over the thing that is ailing and in need of restoration."[1]

Singing has always been used as a restorative aid to bring healing to the suffering. The Winnebago from Michigan lake country tend to the wounded by singing songs obtained from the power of the bear spirits.[2] David healed King Saul with his harp and song. Navajos restore their patients to health through sandpaintings and song.

All over the world people use song for healing. This ancient form of restoring well-being has begun to surface again in the western world. Hopefully, we can learn from cultures who never lost the power of song. For Westerners, I believe that the return of sound healing will be an important aspect of medicine in the future.

I don't know how song heals, I know that it does. When I say heal, I do not mean cure. While a cure may be a by-product of healing, the focus resides elsewhere. Healing brings wholeness out of a shattered state. A person returns to harmony with themselves and their world. Hidden within our language are metaphors which describe the connection between music and health.

We are made up of sound. Every atom, every cell has a vibration. Every organ has a tone. Every body system has a rhythm. To be alive means to have a pulse. To be "sound" means to be healthy. To be well is to be in harmony with one's surroundings, to be "in tune." When our muscles are strong they are well-toned. When we are sick we are out of synch. All of these are musical terms. "If it is considered that each molecule of which an organ or a tissue is composed has its own individual sound pattern, a healthy organ will have its molecules working together in harmonious relationship with each other."[3]

Our bodies have marvelous and predictable rhythms: heart rhythms, breath rhythms, rhythms pulsing from our brains as beta, alpha, theta and delta rhythms. Our stomachs, kidneys and intestines have their own rhythms. Women's bodies are tuned to a lunar rhythm of 28 days with the menstrual cycle.[4]

We are made up of sound. Dr. Susumo Ohno, a geneticist at the Beckman Research Institute of the City of Hope in Duarte, California has created songs by assigning notes to the nucleotides within DNA. "Listeners knowledgeable about music have taken these DNA-based compositions for the music of Bach, Brahms, Chopin and other great composers. These melodies are majestic and inspiring. Many persons hearing them for the first time are moved to tears: they cannot believe their bodies, which they believed to be mere collections of chemicals, contain such uplifting, inspiring harmonies— that they are musical."[5]

Dr. Ohno also did the reverse. He started with a somber Chopin piece, translated the notes into chemical notations and found that "sections of the resulting formula were the DNA of a human cancer gene."[6] Dr. Larry Dossey believes, "Our nerves, our ganglia, and our cells also vibrate. The law of resonance teaches us: anything that vibrates reacts to vibrations."[7]

Hans Jenny, a Swiss scientist researched the work of German physicist Ernst Chladni for 10 years. Both men found that sound creates matter. (When sand is scattered on a steel disc and a violin is plucked nearby, the disc creates circular, almost cellular forms.) Jenny used liquids, powders and metal filings on discs and created changing forms through the use of sound. These looked like honeycombs, flowers and other organic shapes. "If sand particles can arrangc themselves in the presence of pure musical vibrations, is it not possible that musical vibrations, made by musical instruments or our own voice, can have an effect on how the cells of our body are arranged?"[8]

Sound can heal as well as destroy. Consider the everyday sounds that you hear in a city: sirens, jackhammers, horns honking, everyday city noise. Consider the sounds you hear at home: television commercials, vacuum cleaners, blenders, telephones, everyday household noise. Consider the everyday sounds of shopping: the high pitched buzzing of fluorescent lights in discount stores, the sounds of cash registers, and the sounds of crowds at the mall. How do these sounds affect our bodies? The song of 20th century techno-crazed culture is a song that produces stress and disease. Steven Halpern, in his book SOUND HEALTH, states that "the ill effects of noise are cumulative… that noise-induced hearing impairment is permanent… and that decibels increase their effect logarithmically."[9]

This means that "while 90 dBA is equal to the sound of a train roaring into a subway station, 100 dBA equals the sound of 10 trains pulling into the station simultaneously. Furthermore, 110 dBA represents 100 trains."[10] Sounds that reach these levels are a jet engine taking off, loud amplified rock music, a power mower, a jackhammer, a chain saw, a game crowd, or a siren. In cities we are bombarded by these sounds on a daily basis. "At 120 dBA…noise reaches the level of pain."[11] In order to be heard in large cities police sirens sound at 122 dBA.[12]

Not only are we in danger of damage to our ears, but to our entire bodies. Noise may create problems with high blood pressure as well as other stress-related diseases, such as ulcers, gastrointestinal disturbances and a host of other complaints.

Some of us awake in the morning to the abrupt sound of an alarm clock. During sleep the parapsympathetic nervous system becomes dominant; when an alarm goes off the sympathetic nervous system is activated. The "fight or flight" mechanism triggers a reaction. Think of what this does to our bodies over a period of time. How can we remember our dreams? How can a day start in harmony if our first waking moment is one of alarm?

Over the last several years I have had many trips to the dentist. I dread the dentist. What I dread most are the sounds of the drills. One rumbles like a jackhammer and the other has a high-pitched whine. These sounds become particularly distressing as they are heard from inside the head. How many other times do we experience sound in this way? What would the world be like if these drills purred like cats or hummed us to sleep like a lullaby?

I wish I could make the sounds of the drill go away but I can't. Sometimes listening to music helps. Sometimes it doesn't when it's Barbra Streisand and I want to sing along but can't— my mouth is filled with metal tools. So I groan. The first time I did this my dentist became nervous and asked what was wrong. "What's wrong? You have a jackhammer in my mouth!" I told him about toning. I explained that when I am uncomfortable I breathe a little deeper and groan. Groan, not scream. I'll save screaming for when a nerve is hit. Groaning helps; the pain and fear lessen. I'm sure my dentist has some interesting stories about me.

After seeing the dentist I hum with my teeth together. This helps replace the intensity of the drill noise with my own lullaby. The vibration eases the gums and tissues. I've noticed it takes less time for the uncomfortable numbing of the anesthetic to wear off.

In my work as a music therapist, I have worked with clients who have cancer and receive chemotherapy. I've worked with people who face surgery. It amazes me that I have to teach people how to groan when they are in pain from an invasive procedure. We are taught "to bite the bullet", "to grin and bear it", "to keep a stiff upper lip". We are too afraid of others' opinions of us to show that we are afraid. When I take my cats to the veterinarian, they meow, hiss and howl. I believe we also have animal reactions inside but cover it over with "civilized" behavior. We think we shouldn't act like children, we are not supposed to cry— or howl. When we follow this assumption, we hold in our pain and create further stress for ourselves.

My husband is a massage therapist and he reports that few of his clients groan when he massages a tense muscle. He, too, has to teach his clients how to let out sounds. These groans in response to discomfort do not need to be loud. It is enough to breathe into the place that hurts and send the breath out with a low tone. This releases the stress.

I have found groaning to be an essential aspect of healing with the voice. Groaning gives voice to the distress. It is the honest sound of a body in pain. When you breathe into the pain it is as if the breath gathers up the tension and releases it through sound. The quality of the pain is similar to the quality of the sound. People may be afraid of being out of control if they make a sound. Contrary to being out of control, this is a way of gaining some control over an uncomfortable situation.

The Bible lists several references about groaning in order to heal. "Twice during the events surrounding Lazarus' death, Jesus spontaneously groaned in what appeared to be a way of centering himself before his prayer to God to bring Lazarus back to life. (John 11:*33, 38*). Various translations of this passage describe this act of Jesus as 'groaning within himself', 'groaning in the spirit', 'being deeply moved in Spirit', and 'with a sigh that came straight from the heart'."[13]

There are many ways to use the voice as a healing instrument. One way is to sing to an ailing person. Perhaps you were sung to as a child when you were sick and remember the comfort and healing that this brought. Laurel Elizabeth Keyes describes another way to use the voice for healing. "When one has a pain somewhere in the body one begins toning as low as the voice can reach, and slowly raises the pitch, as a siren sound rises. One will find there is a tone which resonates with the pain and relieves the tension."[14]

Some sound healers use vocal sounds to vibrate different parts of the body. The Chinese have developed *chi gung* exercises which use specific sounds combined with movement to correspond with the organs of the body.

Physical healing has sometimes been a by-product of toning. Sometimes clients or students will say that they came in with a headache or other pain and after the toning they notice it is gone. Groaning and toning are not a cure-all. They are a natural human response to pain and brings comfort.

A healing technique which I learned from music therapist Helen Bonny is simple and can be used with groups; it has wonderful results:

> One person lies down on a mat on the floor. Other participants circle around the person who is asked whether he or she would like to be touched. If the person would like touch, participants begin to place their hands on different parts of the body. Typical places touched are over the heart, solar plexus, head, joints, and feet. The person in the center can request specific places where they would appreciate touch, as well as places they would not like to be touched. It is important that the touch be firm and steady, not stroking. The group then listens to the person in the center. They listen for a note, the

note needed by that person at that moment. Whoever hears the note sounds it. Others join in by singing the note in unison and then varying the sounds to include perfect fifths and octaves. The person in the center receives these sounds. The entire experience lasts between five or ten minutes. Usually the face of the central person goes through visible changes. The face softens. Some glow. Smiles spread. Tears can flow.

People who have received this form of treatment have felt instantly relaxed, almost a profound peace. Something melts away. One woman remarked that she felt as if she was inside a flower. A man said the voices sounded angelic. Many heard the same note sounding inside them before it was sung. This simple process amazes me. It often feels like we are part of an archaic procedure. We really do know how to listen to each other's spirit. Touch, sound and loving intent are powerful ingredients.

In one of my classes, a pregnant woman attended whose baby was in a breech position. During the toning she began to feel very hot and felt a lot of activity from the baby. Several days later, an examination confirmed that her baby had turned toward a normal position. The mother believed something happened as she sang that allowed the baby to turn.

Another dramatic example of toning and healing was with a client who came in needing to relax after a stressful week. She had laryngitis. She reclined on a mat and I led her through a deep relaxation. I began to tone the sounds I heard as I listened to her. First, some hoarse sounds emerged followed by clear tones. After the session she spoke in a clear voice. Her laryngitis was gone and did not return. I do not know logically or scientifically how this was done. Kay Gardner believes that "toning enables sound to permeate the body, vibrating the imbalanced areas and affecting a restructuring of the molecules in dis-eased area."[15]

The power of the human voice to heal another is profound. It is time to reawaken and reclaim this very old and very new method to work with suffering. In the future, sound healing will be an important and respected component of medicine. I truly believe that the human voice will be recognized as an integral ingredient toward achieving wellness.

Opening quote: Sufi Inayat Khan, *Music*, Sufi Publishing Co., New Delhi, India, 1962, p. 92.

1. Clarissa Pinkola Estes, *Women Who Run With The Wolves: Myths and Stories of the Wild Woman Archetype*, Ballantine Books, New York, 1992, pp. 27-28.
2. Paul Radin, "Music and Medicine Among Primitive People", in Dorothy M. Schullian and M. Schoen (eds.), *Music and Medicine,* Schuman, New York, 1948, p. 17.
3. Peter Guy Manners quoted in Kay Gardner, *Sounding the Inner Landscape: Music as Medicine,* Caduceus Pub., Stonington, Maine, 1990, p. 125.
4. Ibid., p. 77.
5. Larry Dossey, MD, "The Body as Music", in Don Campbell (ed.), *Music and Miracles*, Quest Books, Wheaton, Illinois, 1992, p. 56.
6. Ibid.
7. Joachim-Ernst Berendt, *Nada Brahma The World is Sound: Music and the Landscape of Consciousness,* Destiny Books, Rochester, Vermont, 1987, p. 40.
8. Steve Halpern with Louis Savary, *Sound Health: The Music and the Sounds That Make us Whole,* Harper and Row, San Francisco, 1985, p. 37.
9. Ibid., pp. 12-13.
10. Ibid., p. 13.
11. Ibid., p. 14.
12. Ibid., p. 12.

13. Ibid., p. 170.
14. Laurel Elizabeth Keyes, *Toning: The Creative Power of the Voice,* Devorss and Company, Santa Monica, California, 1973, p. 34.
15. Kay Gardner, *Sounding the Inner Landscape: Music as Medicine,* Caduceus Publications, Stonington, Maine, 1990, p. 36.

Final Voices

"Return again
Return to the land of your soul
Return to who you are
Return to what you are
Return to where you are
Born and reborn again."
Ronnie Kahn

All over the earth people use song during various stages of death and the grieving process. Song helps both the dying and the living cope with letting go of the earthly body.

In Ireland professional mourners called "keeners" let loose loud wailing sounds that help the family and friends of the deceased let go of their own grief through crying and sobbing.[1]

In Nevada the Pauites hold Cry Dances, dancing and chanting throughout the night while holding strips of the deceased's clothing. The spouse steps before the coffin and the night is filled with her cry; "the sad terrible sound of human grief is a lonely, proud, noble, almost cosmic lamentation."[2] Others support the spouse's lament with their own voices.

In the Kaluli tribe of New Guinea weeping moves women to song. As they weep, their songs show their feelings about loss, death and abandonment.[3]

Song belongs to the mystery of life. Breathing in we inspire. Breathing out we expire. Song rides on the long exhalation. It requires letting go. A residual vibration in song creates a palpable atmosphere around us that we experience. Those at the death bed of a loved one often feel a lingering of the life force; they remain until it slowly fades.

Therese Schroeder-Sheker sings to the dying as a musical-sacramental midwife. Her Chalice of the Repose project in Montana offers training on how to attend the dying through music and song. She describes a death when she tended a man in his eighties who was dying of emphysema. As he struggled for breath she sang Gregorian chants into his ear. "He rested in my arms and began to breathe much more regularly, and we, as a team, breathed together. It was as if the way in which sound anointed him now made up for the ways in which he had never been touched or returned touch while living the life of a man. The chants seemed to bring him balance, dissolving fears and compensating for those issues still full of sting. How could they do anything less?"[4]

"The new midwife," she says, "is a chalice, and sings with bright longing for the simultaneous reception of spirit and matter, humanity and divinity."[5] She stays after the death holding vigil while "they quietly, almost invisibly, shimmer an indescribable membrane of light."[6]

Song provides a road for the departed soul to travel upon. It acts as a bridge between the worlds, of heaven and earth. Can you imagine how different our world would be if we all departed this body on a path of song? How different it would be if the last thing you heard was not the sounds of a hospital room but the sound of someone singing to you. Just as it is the first sense to develop, hearing is the last sense to leave. We hold onto it longest as we make the transition from this plane to the next. Dying people often report hearing voices of departed loved ones or angels singing just before they die. How might each death be more consciously assisted if someone was present to ease the pain, to encourage you to follow the music you hear into the other realm, to continue to sing for you as your soul departs?

Schroeder-Sheker says the song becomes warmth that "helps someone slip from a body of pain into a birth canal."[7] This song is for the dying and for the living. It is the "turning point when you can see that you must die to things every moment so that you can continually warm to life and living and experience the Resurrection... This burning transforms your body, soul and spirit and also becomes unbearable unless you give your voice away."[8] To attend a dying person in this way is an act of love.

I was called one day to sing to a comatose woman who was dying. Her brother lived in another state and couldn't be with her. He asked me to sing for her and the family. I honored his request and also told him to sing for his sister because she was in a place that recognized no time or distance. From some part of herself she would hear him.

When I got to the hospital, I met with the family and told them I was there to sing. I felt as if we already knew each other. We talked about what I would sing, some favorite songs of the dying woman that had meaning to her. One sister tearfully said that the singing "would help me say goodbye."

Knowing comatose patients can hear, I introduced myself to the dying woman and told her I was there to sing for her at her brother's request. I also told her that he would be singing for her as well. I asked her to use the song in any way she needed for her healing. Her family joined hands around her and also placed a hand on her as I sang. The sounds of their weeping accompanied my songs.

As I drove home I wept, wondering about the cycles of life and death and of my connection to this family, whom I met only once during a time of great love and loss.

The next morning I received a call from her brother telling me that his sister had died. He thanked me for singing and told me his own story. As he was singing he felt a strong connection to his sister. The full moon was rising just as the sun was setting. The moment he stopped singing he got the call that told him his sister had died. He was filled with awe as he told his story.

Many fairy tales and myths speak of songs connected to death. Didn't Orpheus persuade Hades, King of the Underworld, to relinquish Eurydice through his song? The song of Orpheus had the power to move Death's King to tears.

"The Nightingale", by Hans Christian Anderson, tells a similar story.[9] After the Emperor of China banishes a real nightingale from his kingdom in favor of a mechanical bird, terrible troubles begin. The clockwork nightingale sings a perfect clockwork song, but when the bird breaks down the Emperor's health begins to fail. Death comes to claim the Emperor's crown and scepter. As he lies on his deathbed he hears voices reminding him of his life's failings. When the real nightingale is told that the Emperor is dying she flies to his bedside and sings. Death listens. The nightingale sings of the quiet graveyard whose grass is green from a watering of freshly fallen tears. Death is entranced and asks the nightingale to keep singing. She continues her song on the condition that Death will lay down the Emperor's crown and scepter. Death does as the nightingale asks and slips out the window. The emperor is restored to health through the power of love's song. If we don't learn to sing with the authentic voice of our life how will Death receive us?

Plains Indians kept the life-death mystery alive through the death chant. Received from a dream, a vision quest or a medicine man, the death chant became a vehicle for connecting with the Great Mystery throughout the stresses and tests of life. "It created a familiarity with the unfamiliar, with death."[10] The death chant was sung at the moment of death, giving life's breath through song back to the Creator.

Schroeder-Sheker has worked with the dying in groups and individually. She remarks, "It has taken a long time to witness a dying group who so fully participate in the creation of biography, the witness of bodily dissolution, transfiguration, epiphany and transition, that they want to sing themselves out, like Thomas Aquinas and his swan song, 'Adore te devote'."[11]

To die singing! To pass into death through song! I can think of no better way to die.

Let it be beautiful when I sing the last song
Let it be day
I would stand with my two feet singing,
I would look upward with my eyes singing,
I would have the winds envelop my body,
I would have the sun to shine upon my body,
Let it be beautiful when Thou wouldst slay me,
O Shining One,
Let it be day when I sing the last song.[12]

Opening quote: Ronnie Kahn in *Circle of Song: Songs, Chants, and Dances for Ritual and Celebration,* compiled by Katie Marks, Full Circle Press, Lenox, Massachussetts, 1993, p. 225.

1. Leah Maggie Garfield, *Sound Medicine: Healing With Music, Voice and Song,* Celestial Arts, Berkeley, 1987, p. 25.
2. Evelyn Eaton, *I Send A Voice*, Quest Books, Wheaton, Illinois, 1978, p. 159.
3. Steven Feld, *Sound and Sentiment: Birds, Weeping, Poetics and Song in Kaluli Expression,* University of Pennsylvania Press, Philadelphia, 1982, p. 33.
4. Therese Schroeder-Sheker, "Musical-Sacramental-Midwifery: The Use of Music in Death and Dying," Don Campbell (ed.), from *Music and Miracles,* Quest Books, Wheaton, Illinois, 1992, p. 20.
5. Ibid., p. 23.
6. Ibid., p. 21.
7. Ibid., p. 23.
8. Ibid.
9. Hans Christian Anderson, *The Nightingale*, Crown Publishers, New York, 1985.
10. Steven Levine, *Who Dies*, Anchor Press/Doubleday, Garden City, New York, 1982, p. 26.
11. Therese Schroeder-Sheker, "Musical-Sacramental-Midwifery: The Use of Music in Death and Dying," Don Campbell (ed.), from *Music and Miracles*, Quest Books, Wheaton, Illinois, 1992, p. 32.
12. Hartley Burr Alexander from Evelyn Eaton, *I Send A Voice,* Quest Books, Wheaton, Illinois, 1978, pp. 162-163.

Verse II

Silenced Voices

"Maybe we're hurt and just can't answer back,
then we sing or maybe even hum the blues.
Yes, to us the blues are sacred.
When I sing . . . what I'm doing
is letting my soul out."
Alberta Hunter

When did we forget to sing? I heard this question asked by a 65-year-old woman who came to one of my singing groups and I have been thinking about it ever since. Perhaps we forgot to sing when television entered our lives and we began to rely on entertainment rather than ourselves for expression. Perhaps we began to compare our voices with the chosen few who sing on stage or across our TV screens. Singing has become big business— if our voices can't earn us a living, then why bother?

Perhaps we forgot to sing when we no longer lived in tribal societies or village life and abandoned the rituals, always accompanied by song, central to the community. As we became more industrialized, requirements for a paycheck presided over our activities, rather than an integrated spiritual life. The steady rhythm of chanting while working gave way to Muzak. The gods no longer accompanied us to our work places and singing became forgotten or forbidden on the job.

Or perhaps the reasons are emotional. We're told not to sing at the table, people look askance at us if we sing in public— singing is somehow "crazy." Singing forms emotional expression and in Western culture we repress our emotions. Perhaps the atomic bomb took our voices when it first mushroomed on the face of the earth. Perhaps the horror of the Holocaust took our voices. Or has rape, incest and child abuse taken away our voices? Perhaps the voice locked itself inside because we felt unsafe to scream or cry out. The tight throat which held back pain was a way to avoid more harm. Self-expression takes place with the awareness that it's safe to let the voice out from behind its veil, to let emotions begin to flow, to allow the body to feel again.

In my work as a music therapist I have found several methods useful in helping people transcend their personal fears of voicing. These include listening to the fears, toning, call and response singing, voice mirroring, simple rounds and chants, imagery techniques, storytelling and establishing an open, non-judgmental atmosphere.

The freeing process involves many things: time, patience, support, physical relaxation, removing physical and emotional blocks, breath awareness, change in attitude and non-judgmental witnessing. Before we can find our true voice, we must first encounter the many voices of people who discounted us. Layers and layers of voices: teachers, parents, siblings, peers— all those who laughed, all those who said "SHUT UP", all those who told us not to scream, not to sing, all those who ridiculed our thoughts and feelings. Voices of abusers, silencers and critics are often internalized. And though these people may no longer exist, they can still silence as remembered messages— secrets must be kept at all costs, messages that our feelings are stupid, messages that no matter what we do we'll never be good enough to measure up. And most devastating of all, we have messages that we deserved this abuse because we are bad to begin with.

Sometimes these voices surface as images. Some are images of black metal chokers around the throat which stop any expression of emotion. We may have images of lids like kitchen sink-stoppers that keep the authentic self from being heard, or images of the mouth being covered by a veil that keeps anything from being said. As these images are slowly and carefully revealed, as they are listened to, the memory and emotion behind the image often surface.

Clients remember the painful details of their abuse. One woman said her father grabbed her by the neck and told her not to cry as he raped her. If she made any sounds he applied more pressure to her throat. Another woman felt like she was screaming behind a glass wall but no one could hear her.

Most of the clients who I have worked with in private practice over the years have been women. Many of them were sexually, physically and/or emotionally abused and had vocal blocks related to the abuse. These are some stories of women who found the courage to break the silence and give voice to their souls:

• A woman has been silenced by her husband and by the courts. There is much anguish. She is not believed when she tells them her child was molested by an older step-son. She witnesses this child molesting her youngest child. The cycle of incest is being repeated because no one will listen to her. She is made out to be exaggerating. Or crazy. Her response is to hold her breath. If she breathes in, there is too much pain. If she breathes out, her words are not believed. If she breathes out, her sobs cannot be contained. She is silenced, powerless to do anything to protect her children who visit the elder sibling on court-appointed visits. Her experience of her voice is sharp and cutting or black and empty. No song can emerge from the anguish of her experience. She cried at not being able to sing. As I mirrored her pain with my voice, this sharp blackness diminished inside her throat. As I gently offered supportive touch to the front of her throat and back of her head she began to breathe more freely. In this moment I offered my comfort, my compassion, my own voice. The rest of the world, the legal system, the mediators had chosen to ignore her. My voice said that "I am listening. I hear you."

• A client arrives to a singing session to work on her own incest and her son's incest by an ex-husband. She has temporal mandibular joint pain from the held-in anger. Her jaw and teeth feel like cold rock, like the crust of a mountain.

"Something wants to crack through and grow." She voices her grief at her son's pain and her anger at her ex-husband and her parents. She voices the pain in her jaw and explores another layer of the tightness. "AUGHHH", she tones loudly and painfully.

I ask her if there is anything in the room that speaks to her that she would like to have with her as she continues to tone through the layers of pain. She takes an ear of Indian corn from the bookshelf and shakes it like a rattle. It makes a rustling sound like fire. She stands and shakes the corn husks and wails "AUGGHHHHHHHH."

She takes a stand against the abuse. Her voice grows more powerful. First, she is angry. Then sad. Sounds of old grief emerge. As her sounds come to an end she says she felt that shaking the corn helped her with her boundaries. She felt small against a raging fire and the sound of the corn, as she waved it in front of her like a rattle, helped to contain her. "I have no mother. I have no father. I ask the earth and grandmother moon to support me. I ask the elements of the earth to help me grow." In that moment she was able to feel the earth and moon, the ancient feminine force, assisting her.

• This same client arrives in physical pain after oral surgery which she has had done several days before. There is pain in her jaw, teeth, gums, mouth and throat. I ask her to place her hands on her jaw and to hum slowly and gently. As she hums she feels soothed. She says it is like singing to the child inside her. "Sleep child." Yes. Make up a song to the child inside who has been in pain. Together we write the song. I write down her words and encourage her to find a tune. She sings softly:

"Weep child
Cry your tears now
Weep child
Cry your tears out

Sleep child
Go to sleep child
Sleep child
Go to sleep now

Dream child
Dream your dreams child
Dream child
Dream your dreams now

Wake child
Wake to morning
Wake child
Love the day now

Laugh child
Shout your laughter
Laugh child
Shout your laughter now

Dance child
Dance your joyful dance
Dance child
Dance the circle now."

"I once wanted this part of me just to go to sleep and not bother me. But I no longer wish to numb myself. I want to have all of my feelings, be able to rest from them and wake to a new day."

• A woman comes in to work with her problems of shame and vulnerability related to her incest as a child. As she tones sounds of grief on *ohhhhhs* and *ahhhhhs* she rubs the moonstone bracelet she wears on her wrist. She rubs this like a talisman. She rocks back and forth toning and rubbing the moonstones. Gradually the sounds of grief give over to sounds of hope, as if the moonstones transmitted something to her as she rubbed them. As she ends she opens her eyes and tells me about her moonstones.

Another therapist she works with suggested that the bracelet is like her badge of courage. As she continues to smooth the moonstones under her fingers she tells me that they are the repository of faith when she feels lost. She feels the circle of moonstones as a circle of protection, the moonstones remind her of all the people she has told about the incest. They are a reminder of the beauty and strength of her voice. They remind her that she has shared this beauty with other people. The moonstones tell her she is beautiful. Even though there is a voice inside that says she is vile, the moonstones speak another truth. She names the people she has shared her beauty with. She names the people she has told her story to. Her moonstones remind her of another truth. "It's like there's a little religion wrapped around my wrist." The moonstones weave together the dark with the light. She says "the essence of a woman is to weave a little bit of dark and a little bit of light and to make a life out of it."

• A woman returns from a week-long vacation by the ocean. "It was miserable, the whole trip was miserable." Her husband had gotten sick, the weather was cold, the food bad. She says she plans and plans their different trips but each turns out miserable. "What is it that you are trying to get away from that comes along with you?" I ask. "The pain," she says. The pain of incest. She has an image of an abandoned child.

She tells me a dream she had of a Mexican man who gives her three birds for safekeeping. One bird flies away. She places the other birds in her mouth. She forgets about them. Later in the dream she sees the birds soaked with water and wadded up on the ground, barely alive. She wonders whether they can survive. The man entrusted the birds to her for safekeeping and now they are wet and lifeless on the ground. They are grounded.

I suggest we make a nest for the birds. She picks a bright purple cloth. I hold the nest for the two wet birds with a space for the third bird to return if it so needs or wants. She begins to sing to the birds but her tears stop her. She has an image of a collapsed child who wants to be in the nest with the birds.

She sings *"ahhhhhhhhs"*, mixing this with sounds of grieving; she sings through tears. Salt tears flow down her face. I support her voice with my own. Her body contracts tighter and tighter and the sounds become a wailing. I vary her sounds with *"shuuuuuuuu shuuuuuuuu ah shu"*, sounds to mother her. She begins to relax. She listens and soaks up the sound, then gently adds her own voice.

As she opens her eyes, she describes how she imagined the nest floating on ocean waves, the birds and the child are being gently rocked, held up by the arms of the ocean.

"Even though the trip was bad— the flame of my faith keeps me strong." She says that the child is the keeper of the flame but she is the one who needs it most.

"Is there a way to bring light to this child?" I ask. She imagines a procession of people— many, many people with an innocence about them. They approach the edge of the water, a procession of the innocent bearing torches. She sings a Hebrew lullaby, both soothing and celebrational. A chorus of voices joins her, singing to the nested birds and the child rocked gently by the waves. She realizes that this is what her child-self needs. She needs to be near others, but to be safely out of reach, rocked in the arms of Mother Ocean. She can feel both the touch of light and the embrace of water. She says, "I'm not alone, we're not alone, we are one, there is healing, we are not alone." I first echo and then sing in unison, harmonizing with her words. She sings the Hebrew lullaby again, her voice growing strong and triumphant. With a radiant smile, she opens her eyes and describes the child and herself dancing together among this procession of the innocent.

I wonder if the birds are dancing, too. No. They are still in the nest. Still wet. But not quite as wet. They have been able to take in warmth from the light and from the song. It is dark now. They need the sunrise. "Is there a safe place to put the nest until you see them again?" I wonder. She places the purple cloth nest underneath my art supply table with her teddy bear left to warm the nest with its body, one eye looking protectively out into the room.

How many of us have birds stuffed in our mouths, keeping us from speaking because we have to keep secrets safe from flying out of our mouths? Our spirits are dampened and nearly dead when secrets are kept in our mouths.

• Can we give birth to ourselves through our voices? One client birthed herself in this way. As she toned, she noticed a tightness and hoarseness in her throat. I asked her if she could look inside her throat to this place of tightness. She noticed a child's head crowning. What sound can you make to help birth this baby, I asked.

She toned, "Ah" and felt the resonance in her throat and the child looking up at her with big brown eyes. "The child is responding to the sound. The sound feels like home. There's an answering to the call." As she continued to call the child out with her tones, she saw the shoulders emerging. She then became very surprised that what she had birthed was "a full-sized me. This form is me but doesn't hold the pattern of all the abuse!" As she toned to this image of her new self she felt a core of resonance between them. "I can feel connections between the new me with my solar plexus, heart and throat." She felt a spiritual connection to this image of her core self.

If we listen deeply enough to another we can hear sounds inside. We can hear sounds of distress, sounds of grief, sounds of pain, and sounds of joy. Some are sounds that have been repressed because it isn't polite to groan in public, to laugh too loudly, or to wail in grief. We have been enculturated away from the sighs, yawns and groans that are part of our natural human response to our world. Sometimes we are so numbed to our emotions and so caught up in the cultural trance that we can't even hear ourselves, much less give voice to what we feel.

There are times in my sessions that I listen deeply for what I hear inside of a client. I listen beyond words to the primal sounds within. I listen for my "sound response" to his or her story. Sometimes my response comes in the form of tones, first toning the distress I hear inside, and then toning what I perceive to be my client's pattern of wholeness, the sounds that are needed to heal. Sometimes I hear a song I know. I hear the words inside myself and sing them. Sometimes what I hear is a song that is unique to the moment or unique to our shared relationship.

• As one woman voiced her pain and anguish of not knowing who she was, of not knowing how to even find the way to herself, I made up a song and sang to her:

Show me the way to myself
Show me the way to myself

Show me the way to myself
I want to know who I am

Lord, show me the way to myself
Show me the way to myself
Show me the way to myself
I want to know who I am

I've been on this road such a long long time
And I want to know who I am
I've been on this road such a long long time
And I want to know who I am

I sang with the same feeling as spirituals, crying out of a deep despair to be heard, singing it as a prayer, as a hope. As I sang my client wept and was comforted in the warm embrace of the song.

• Over a period of years I worked with a woman who was adopted. She had questions about her origin. She was a woman who had difficulty expressing her feelings and she felt abandoned. She was a singer with a beautiful voice who sang in choirs and ensembles, but she didn't know how to sing her own story. She had access to vocal techniques, and much practice in singing but somehow there was a block to her deeper voice, her true self.

One day, as we worked together with toning, I thought her sounds were pretty, but I felt there was something underneath that called for expression. I asked her if I could make the sounds I was hearing. As I toned, something opened up in both her voice and her memory. She had a copper taste in her mouth. She remembered when she was very small she used to wet the bed. Every morning her bed was dry, her adopted father gave her a 1958 penny, the year she was born. When he left the room she swallowed the penny. She had seen people put pennies in piggybanks. Somewhere in her child's mind she thought, since money was valuable, if she swallowed the pennies she would be valuable too.

Her throat felt as it had at five years old when she swallowed pennies. She had completely forgotten this experience. She stood up and sang in a radiant voice full with feeling. She connected her emotions with her body through her voice in a way that she had never been able to do before. She gave value to herself through her own song.

Opening quote: Alberta Hunter, quote from *The Brad Kelly Radio Show.*

At the Well of Silence

"There is a balm in Gilead that heals the wounded soul."
African-American Spiritual

Silencing can take many forms. Even in the face of being silenced healing can occur. I learned a profound lesson about silencing and silence when I was asked to lead morning devotionals and an ending ceremony at the Women's Wellness Conference held annually at Ghost Ranch in Abiquiu, New Mexico. The day before the conference began, I woke up with a sinus infection and laryngitis, a fever made my mind blank.

I looked at the brochure— "Susan Elizabeth Hale will lead early morning devotionals. Using sacred music from many traditions we will greet the day with toning and chanting. We will enter a candlelit room into an atmosphere of music. Gentle movement may accompany some songs." Songs! What songs? I can't even speak!

And if this wasn't enough dilemma, I had titled the ending ceremony— "Birthing Our Voices to the World." What kind of midwife can I be with no voice? I try to call the organizer of the conference to back out, but she's not home. My body says, "Don't be heroic. Stay home. Rest. Take care of yourself." Wise words I would usually listen to. But instead, I call up a friend who is a holistic healer as well as a registered nurse. She hears my desperate plea. I had hoped she would tell me to stay home. No such luck. She says that even though I have physical symptoms, she feels the real cause is of a spiritual nature. She asks me if anything in the last few days has triggered this. I think back and remember being moved by a client who had suffered terrible abuse. This client had most wanted to be a singer, yet was too blocked to utter a sound.

My friend thought that this might have affected an old residue of fear inside myself. I was reminded of a recurring dream-memory of a Middle Eastern woman whose tongue gets cut off for speaking undesirable truths. She asked me if I can imagine a healing ritual. I saw a well in the desert with women singing to me and bathing me in rose petals. So she suggested that I repeat a mantra: "I am truth, I am life, I am love. Blessed are those who follow the voice. Blessed are those who look within to deep places." I realize that going to Ghost Ranch is important even if my voice doesn't return.

The next morning I wake up to a tight, raw place in my throat. As I try to speak, only a hoarse imitation of my voice emerges. I pack half-heartedly, still not sure about attending this four day conference. As I pack I see a pink scarf which reminds me of roses. Something inside me says "If you don't go you'll be giving up to forces of repression. You need to go and sing your song even without a voice."

As I drive there I repeat my mantra. "I am truth. I am life. I am love. Blessed are those who follow the voice. Blessed are those who look within to deep places." I sing in my mind on the highway, through Santa Fe, Española, to Abiquiu and finally to the dirt road leading to Ghost Ranch. Arriving there is like driving into an oasis of lush green fields, huge old cottonwoods, all surrounded by towering red mesas and 360 degrees of sweeping mountain vistas. As I see Kitchen Mesa and Chimney Rock I feel welcomed. I feel as if I am cradled inside a pink rose. I remember the very first time I visited I heard a choir singing *"There is a balm in Gilead"* from the Convocation Hall. This memory greeted me as an affirmation of a healing. I had made the right choice.

After settling in, my roommate and I walk over to an evening performance of "Georgia O'Keefe's New Mexico and Lawrence's Girls"— a one woman play by a Taos playwright/actress which portrayed Georgia O'Keefe, Freida Lawrence, Dorothy Brett, and Mable Dodge Luhan. The play reveals that what O'Keefe most wanted to be was a singer. Since she didn't feel adequate as a singer, she brought forth inner music through her paintings.

I go to sleep quietly chanting my mantra. Morning comes and still no voice. I'm grateful for my collection of instruments: ocharinas, Tibetan bowl, chimes, rattles, drums. I'm grateful for a tape recorder and my tapes. For my ceremony I light a candle, and go outside playing my drum, letting it be my voice to call women to the devotional. One by one they gather into a group of twenty. We form a circle. I play an ocharina in the shape of a frog and whisper that my intention was to sing beautiful songs, but, alas, I have a frog in my throat. I explain that my instruments and tapes will have to be my voice. I quietly speak the chant "The Earth is our Mother we must take care of her… Her sacred ground we walk upon with every step we take" and then ask everyone to be mindful as we walk to the Hall. Inside, I mouth the words and use my hands as an indication for everyone to sing. As they sing, some close their eyes in meditation. With the help of a tape, I teach "Oh Great Spirit, earth and wind and sea, you are inside and all around me", teaching sign language movements of the words. I teach the Basque song *"O Shoo Wa"*, a song to cleanse the heart, a song which has a whispered section. I whisper instructions on how to tone. I cannot model this with my own voice as I normally would, so the group tones softly and serenely. I end by playing the Tibetan bowl near each woman so she can hear the subtle overtones. I ask everyone to take the peace of this morning with them and to remember the sacredness of the Earth, even as they walk the linoleum floors of the Dining Hall.

Somehow, everything felt right. In spite of, or because of, my physical ills I felt that deep well of spirit radiating from me. Uniquely me, but also more. Without a voice I allowed my essence to sing. Without a voice I was able to be heard. I knew that nothing could ever silence me.

When I returned to my room, my friend handed me a copy of a small book, Circle of Stones. As I opened it to read I was immediately struck by these words:

> "An old woman, her shoulders wrapped in a
> grey woolen shawl spoke softly:
> I ask, what is asked of us? And answer comes…
> to come, each of us, to our own voice…
> our own feminine voice…
> What is asked of us? To find a voice… a voice
> to cry out… to make us all attend to our woundedness,
> our pain, our anguish, our needs… in ourselves, our
> children, our men, in nature itself… that

vast woundedness which has been so ignored, so denied...
to attend that woundedness, and at last to honor it...
the woundedness of us all...
in hope and faith that it may heal."[1]

I thought of the Middle Eastern woman in my memory. I heard cries. I saw her bathed in rose petals. I breathed in the scent of those roses.

The next morning I was surprised to see over thirty women present for the devotional. Still with no voice I spoke my truth and let my spirit sing. I felt transparent. On the last day, there were fifty women who came to chant, cry, and sing. I could palpably feel their voices bathing me as they toned. During the last toning my voice suddenly returned. A new vibration resonated from my voice. Something magical had happened and I was filled with a profound sense of humility and gratefulness for the mystery and healing found in the well of silence.

Opening quote: African American spiritual, public domain.

1. Judith Duerk, *Circle of Stones: Woman's Journey to Herself*, Lura Media, San Diego, 1989, p. 64.

Women's Voices

"It is holy poetry and singing that we are after. We want powerful words and songs that can be heard under water and over land. It is the wild singing we are after, our chance to use the wild language we are learning by heart under the sea. When a woman speaks her truth, fires up her intention and feeling, stays tight with the instinctive nature, she is singing, she is living in the wild-breath stream of her soul."

Clarissa Pinkola Estes

One day I drove into town to take my car in for an emissions test. I waited in a line of other cars for an hour on a busy street corner. Traffic whizzed past. Horns honked. Radios blared. Sirens screamed. Engines idled. The man in the emissions testing booth was playing the radio. As I got closer it became louder. I rolled up my windows and sang, trying to stay within my own vibration rather than be assaulted by all the noise, but the sounds outside were too loud, too intrusive, too constant. Finally after getting into the booth I found out that my car didn't pass. He suggested I might need a tuneup. So I drove to a tuneup-while-you-wait place and sat another hour, again near a busy street and near a blaring radio. I needed a tuneup as well, but I wasn't getting one. I was getting bombarded by city sounds of concrete, metal, high hums of telephone lines, wired sounds of rush. As I watched the traffic and listened to its sounds and the songs on the radio I noticed how one described the other. The beat of the music was like the flow of the traffic. The music sounded fast without really taking you anywhere. The traffic was rushed without really going anywhere. Where are we in such a hurry to go? Why are we going so fast? Why aren't we listening to how we feel when we are subjected to the type of visual and auditory assault that cities breed? "It sounds like the patriarchal war dance that pumps everyone up to keep them aggressive," one man said as he heard my story.

These are electronic sounds of fast rhythmic pulses that keep us wired. The adrenaline keeps us on the move. Keep it pumping. "Pump up the volume." Many of the sounds I heard from car radios were heavy metal and rap music. Much of this music uses a rhythm called a stopped anapestic beat. This beat goes directly against the human heart.

Why are we going against the heart?

While working with children in a psychiatric hospital I gave music therapy sessions to the youngest classroom two days a week. During every session we sang. Helping with the class was an old woman from a nearby pueblo. She wasn't on the professional staff, she was one of the "Grandmas" who came to give extra attention to the children. One day, after I had taught a simple song with movements about planting seeds and falling rain, she followed me back to my office. "That song you sang. It's a sacred song. My people sing and dance to bring the rain to help the seeds grow." She danced in my office and sang a song for me. My song had been to the tune of *"The Farmer in the Dell."* Hers had an ancient tune born of the red earth of New Mexico. Her dancing feet were like a heartbeat. When she was through with her dance she looked at me and said, "You function life with your voice, you function life with your song."

I have often thought about what she said. I ask myself what is it that functions life, functions healing, functions community, functions the heart, functions the earth? And what is it that is dysfunctioning, that goes against the grain, that goes against the heart? We hear so much about dysfunctional families. We go back into the past in therapy rooms to look at the family shadow. But then we leave therapy and go right out into a dysfunctioning world, one that goes against our basic natures. We are held in a cultural trance that operates on a very narrow band of consciousness. Most pop music operates on this narrow band. It doesn't require us to listen, to think, to feel. It hooks us with catchy phrases and a driving beat, but it doesn't take us anywhere. We have pop icons who we make into cultural heroes. We have given over our right to sing.

According to Angeles Arrien, cultural anthropologist and author, when dispirited people in an indigenous culture seek help from a shaman or a medicine-woman they are asked four questions:

1) When did you stop singing?
2) When did you stop dancing?
3) When did you stop being enchanted with stories?
4) When did you first start to feel uncomfortable with deep silence?

To lose these is to lose soul, the connection with our instinctual natures. Nowadays, television and movies give us our songs, dances, and stories. They take away the quiet. They take away the songs, dances and stories that grow out of the deep silence if we were to listen. When we are uncomfortable with our own silence, all we have to do is push a button and the void inside is temporarily filled. But what is it filled with? Yes, there are some wonderful programs, inspiring songs, brilliant actors and sensitive stories. But we have to wade through so much to get to them. And we tend to compare our own attempts at creativity with what we see on television. Much of what we do see is not brilliant, sensitive or inspiring. How many more times do we sit by and watch bodies without heads, without voices, or without feet to stand on, sell cars, cereal, or beer? Where are the ancient rhythms that function life? It's time to wake up and listen to the birds, trees, wind and mountains. We need to listen to the old songs that nature sings. Listen to our bodies, our symptoms, our sensibilities, our sensitivities. We need to listen to what functions life.

To wake up from the "war dance", the Feminine needs to be voiced so that we can find a way to live that nourishes our hearts, souls and communities. Women need to find their voices and deliver that wake-up call to a culture out of balance. To illustrate what the Feminine Voice sounds like, I am including narratives from several sessions of an ongoing women's toning group. These sessions share the magic of what can happen when women get together to sing and give voice to their souls.

The original intention of this book was to be about women's voices. Dreams and conversations encouraged me to broaden this book to be about human voices and the human need to sing. However, these narratives are at the heart of my work. Words are pale echoes for the rich songs we created together. I can't explain what happened in these groups. I can only talk around the process and let the experiences and the women speak for themselves.

• A class member brings in a dream. She's on a boat. Leontyne Price comes on board. They row down the river together and pick up other things. A man says that everything on the boat has been discarded.

As we respond to this dream we notice the theme of the discarded voice, the discarded feminine. How has society discarded our voices? How do we continue to discard ourselves, our words, our thoughts, or our feelings by listening to sources outside of ourselves?

Another class member responds to the dream in song, in affirmation that we are here exploring our voices together to pick up what has been discarded:

Go down the river
Gonna pick up my voice
Go down the river
Gonna pick up my voice
Go down the river
Gonna pick up my voice
Go down the river
Gonna pick up my voice
Hallelujah, I found my voice
Hallelujah I have my voice

As we sing together we make up other verses picking up all those discarded things in our lives that we need to be truly human.

• At another group I read the dialogue from the movie *RAMBLING ROSE* in which the character Mrs. Hilliard confronts her husband and the doctor who want to perform a hysterectomy on Rose for "therapeutic reasons" to "spare her the suffering she causes herself". After confronting them, the doctor becomes sarcastic and assures her the surgeon will be "guided by her wishes." Mrs. Hilliard stands and delivers a stirring reply:

> *"Let him be guided not by my wishes, nor by Rose's wishes, though I'm sure they are identical. Let him be guided by the wishes of the creative power of life itself. Because that is what has spoken through me here today."*[1]

We take our discussion of the movie's image into the reality of our own lives. The creative power of life itself— how can we let it speak through us? Breathe into the power. Allow it to flow through us. To allow it to sing, we first go to the dissonant, grieving, dark places. Images of Inanna, the Sumerian goddess who descended into the underworld, emerge... images of the changing season from light into the beginning darkness of fall ... images of black, rich earth. The sounds continue to clash against each other and then our voices break through— Hi ya ho hi ya ho . . . the rhythmic beat grows in intensity until the sound is drumming through us. The HO, like a drumbeat invokes the power within. We meet in the center with our sounds and then sounds fade gradually. Deep breath. We open our eyes slowly.

One woman grew afraid with the powerful sound of HO which she felt resonating in her abdomen: fear of the power of life, fear of the newness of the feeling. For another woman there was a conscious exploration of dissonance and defiance. Someone had rubbed her the wrong way and she'd taken it and now she wanted to explore sounds against sounds. "I'm letting my bad girl out. Daring to be dissonant like Mrs. Hilliard. Daring to be heard." For another there were images of women around a fire chanting at the dark of the moon, new moon, full moon ... dancing, chanting, raising power with their voices.

We toned again with the suggestion to evoke the strength of the spirit of our mothers, our grandmothers, the ancient lineage of women, to evoke their brazen courage and strength. "But the women in my background were all marshmallows." "No woman who gives birth is a marshmallow," another responded. One woman talked about the strong tough stock of women she came from. Her great grandmother outlived three husbands. "What is our intention in evoking this primal feminine?"

We want to link with this force to help us break through our resistances; to acknowledge our strength and power; to add to the collective feminine; to use our voices for transformation in our cells and beyond our cells. We want all to feel this force.

We breathe into these intentions and the sounds emerge. Sounds that remind us of deep, gnarled roots, rocks, wrinkles, which are ancient, craggy, beneath, everything that has been denied or shunned. Names of goddesses surface... Isis, Kuan Yin, Mary, Inanna, Diana, Gaia, Io, Terra, White Buffalo Woman... they grow out of the sounds, out of our breath, rather than being sung or chanted, they arise from the sounds. And our tones rise up, becoming more rarified, ethereal, radiant. In the center I see an image of a large, very pregnant woman, pregnant with the earth. I'm in awe, in ahhhhhhhhh. The sounds become even lighter, higher, more pure, like stars circling light in the sky, like rays of light streaming from the center. As we grow quiet we are reverent, still vibrating with the pulse of our songs. As we talked we noted the full spectrum of the sounds linking the two aspects of the feminine.

We felt grateful to be part of this mystery. One woman said our singing was like a vocal orgasm. Another felt she was like the tough old women in her family. There was a shared awareness that we've been fragmented and we are now bringing ourselves back together through our voices. One woman felt a place of strength and had images of women working in the fields, giving birth in the fields, the hidden strength of women hiding in harems . . . all these women emerging as part of the power, part of the strength . . . we're continuing in this pattern. Our lives are part of the pattern of women's strength.

• On another night the toning was multi-layered with rhythms and counter-rhythms. Everyone improvised, each was very different, but each was part of the whole. One woman said it was the sound of grieving and letting go of summer, but also a song about fall and its beauties and a preparation for winter. Another felt expansive and forgot about the room, immersed instead with Native American images. She got lost in the song. Three of us heard similar things in the sounds. Variations of the words Holy and Hallelujah. Without saying these actual words this is what we heard through the tones. "It's like being in a holy place. We created this holy place with our voices."

We are women
We are holy
We are women
Hear our voices

No more songless
No more wordless
We are women
Holy singers

We took this feeling into a second toning adding our own words to match the feelings in the room, in our voices and out of the tones came Hallelujah, hear our voices, hear our words, hear our song, heal our souls, Holy heal, Holy Mother, hear our voices, Holy Whole-y, we are healers.

After the toning a deep quiet followed and then one by one each woman spoke:

"I have found a voice in spite of my fear."
"We became the singing."
"My voice has found its feet."
"We went beyond women to soul."

We wondered what it would be like if everyone on earth sang together at the same time, if we could lay down our differences and all sing together— if board meetings and Congress and arms negotiations would begin their meetings with toning and song.

• At another group we talked about fear. Fear as the shadow side of power. We each took a rattle and stated our fears… I fear my fear, r-r-rattle… I fear being left out in the cold, r-r-rattle and others rattled in encouragement… I fear my power, that I'll be the abuser, not the abused, r-r-rattle… I fear being abandoned, r-r-rattle… I fear the disregard for life I read about in the newspapers, r-r-rattle... I fear being sucked down into the mire, r-r-rattle... we took our rattles into voicing sounds of fear, shivering sounds, fearful sounds. Like mice we've been afraid, and out of the sounds came a cry for help. The cry repeated and others joined in the cry ... help... help... help... help me... listen to me... help me... help me... help us... hear us... help us... and this became a prayer... hear us... care for us... reach out... reach out... and as we reached out with our voices we reached out with our hands, reached out to one another so we would not be alone in the fear, alone in the darkness. We reached out to one another and our prayer grew stronger... Lord, hear us... hear our cries... hear our prayers... shield us... protect us... encircle us with your love... protect us... lift our fears... cleanse us... heal us with your love... let us feel your peace... let us feel your spirit... heal us with your love... hear us... heal us... let us feel your strength... let us feel our strength... as we sang our bodies moved round in a circle. We sang for ourselves, we sang for all women, all children, all men, all cultures, all creatures, all those who live in fear and cry for help. We sang and the song was the answer to the prayer. The song gradually came to a close and we remained holding hands for some time, still swaying, safe within the circle of song.

• One woman came in to the group upset. She had just been to dinner with a friend who was in a life-threatening situation. She felt frustrated, tearing-her-hair-out-frustrated. Breathe into it. Breathe into wherever you are tonight. Breathe into whatever you're feeling. Errrraaaaaaaa grrrr ohhhhhhh groans and sounds that sounded like haunted house sounds, tearing, ripping sounds and from the sounds came words of "this and that, this and that... I don't understand... No more... no more... no more denial...

listen… listen to me… listen to what we're saying… listen… we take a stand with our voices… we know what we're saying now… listen… (our voices like drumbeats… like rap)… listen… listen to our feelings… listen… (and we echoed the word— *listen*, first loudly, then more gently)… listen… listen… (the words to an old chant)… listen, listen, listen to my heart song… listen to my heart… listen to my feelings… *listen*…"

When we finished we were energized by what happened. We talked about the importance of taking a stand in the feminine, of saying "NO" to numbness… saying "NO" again and saying it again. One woman said she felt the power of our voices go beyond the room to the street. Taking our song to the streets, that's different than exploring our voices in the safe nest we've created. It is a scary proposition to be a small group of women singing in the streets at night. Especially with the message of— "LISTEN TO US… LISTEN TO OUR FEELINGS… I'M TALKING TO YOU… NO MORE NUMBNESS." We could be a gang, someone suggested. A chanting gang. Instead of graffiti we'd bring song to different sections of the city: board meetings, institutions, court rooms, newsrooms, back alleys, freeway onramps. We'd have jackets with our names on them. "We're gonna tone you up, so tune in and WAKE UP."

The second toning was very different. At first it sounded like a cross between Bing Crosby crooning, razz-ma-tazz and ragtime. It was a rhythmic, jazzy, swing layered with soft brushed drum sounds, crooning melodies, playful but focused. The sounds emerged into words… "I'm walking down the road singing my song" so, whether consciously or not, we are still singing about taking our song to the streets… "I'm walking my walk and talking my talk… I'm walking down the road singing my song… I know who I am, I know who I am . . . we know who we are . . . we know . . . we have a wisdom that comes from deep inside... deep... deep inside... deep inside I know who I am... deep inside... deep, deep within my cells, down deep inside, alive, alive, glad to be alive and I choose life... I choose to shine... let the light shine... let it shine through me... let the light shine through me down to the core... deep down, down to the core." Our voices echoed low, low, very low sounds. Strong and grounded. We ended in this low place together. "It sounded like the sound effects for the journey to the center of the earth." We talked about the transformation of emotion that had occurred since the beginning when one woman had come through the door frustrated and wanted to tear her hair out. There was a tangible transformation in our faces and bodies and voices that we felt vibrating inside. There was a heat and energy generated by our voices that felt like a warm fire glowing in the center of the room. Emotion is energy, if you move it through, something changes. Emotion gets voiced and moved, set in motion: E-motion, e-moting, *E-e-e-e-e-e-e-e-e*, not stuck in one place, but fluid.

We talked about the newness of going so low, feeling the sounds vibrate through the body down to the toes. We explored "how low can you go." We felt this bass place that is often unfamiliar to women's voices. Journey to the center of the earth. We toned earth sounds, imagining places on the earth we wanted to explore— mountains, meadows, forests. Resisting the temptation to imitate what we've heard before... we went inside these images of the earth to hear their sounds and how they spoke to us... we listened to the earth's voice and allow her to voice through us. We started with low sounds, sounds of wind and deep rumblings, sounds of insects, birds which shifted into the vibrations of a clear blue sky... the melody inside trees... indescribable but familiar... the pulsings within rocks, within the earth's core. We ended on a low pulsing sound. After moments of silent reverence, I chanted, "I heard the earth and she said... I heard the earth and she said . . . I heard the earth and she said heal me." Each woman intoned her own words as we went around the circle.

> "I heard the earth and she said I'm grateful for your listening."
> "I heard the earth and she said go inside."
> "I heard the earth and she said uncover."
> "I heard the earth and she said go deeper, go deeper still."
> "I heard the earth and she said I'm here, I'm here, I'm here underneath."
> "I heard the earth and she said I'm singing to you. Sing with me."

The earth had gone inside our voices. There was a moment of quiet awe... of being different voices, each having something to say through song... each distinct, unique, alone but each listening and responding to one another while maintaining integrity and individuality. There was a peacefulness on each woman's face. To end the evening I sang a soft lullaby improvised from the moment. At first the group just listened and soaked up the song. Then softly other voices joined in. When the song finished I looked at each woman and myself and said, "The words of the song are saying do you know how beautiful you are? Do you know? Do you know how beautiful your voices are? Take it in. Take in your beauty. Take in the beauty and strength of all our songs tonight and take it inside to all of those places that need healing." We scooped up the song still vibrating from the center as if it was water to cleanse us. We washed ourselves with the healing balm of music and took the healing that we've experienced tonight out into the world.

In these examples from the toning group, we listen inside, listening for the truth of ourselves and we give this to the group as the truth of who we are in the moment. We receive sounds from others and in our listening, when one singer is inspirited, when a deep honest sound comes at us straight from the soul, there is a magnetizing effect on the rest of the group. The other voices gravitate towards the truth. Toning in this way is like finding the center, finding the center of ourselves through listening and finding the center of the group, adding to that center with our truth. There is a tangible sense that each time we tone this way we are creating something in the center that is greater than the sum of our voices. What we create in the center through the giving of our life's breath through sound feels warm and renewing and is available for the greater good on the planet.

Through this group, the sacred feminine is brought into the world by each of us in her own way. Sometimes in small ways, sometimes in big ways. We do this when we voice something out of our female sensibility without apology to another. Many times there is an apology in our words, tone or attitude because we fear the world won't understand. We discount ourselves as women when we make assumptions that others won't be able to understand, or will laugh at, our experience. When we act out of our knowingness, we give the world a gift. When we sing, share feelings, share our sensitivities and dreams of our inner worlds, share our sentiments, creativity, our unique perception without apology, we bring the sacred feminine to a world in need of these experiences. The world needs more sensitivity. The world needs more people to share dreams, images and feelings. The world is thirsty for the sacred. When we share in this way— everything is at the level of honor, where heaven meets earth.

We took this into our last toning, taking our sounds to the level of honor. As we ended, one woman continued to sing alone, a song she sings in her morning meditation. She sang sweetly. Slowly and softly we joined her. Her song sounded like a prayer. We sang and the song was the answer to the prayer.

Opening quote: Clarissa Pinkola Estes, *Women Who Run With The Wolves,* Ballantine Books, New York, 1992, p. 291.

1. Rambling Rose, Carolco Pictures, 1991, screenplay by Calder Willingham.

Men's Voices

"The growth of a man can be imagined as a power that gradually expands downward; the voice expands downward into the open vowels that carry emotion, and into the rough consonants that are like gates holding that water; the hurt feelings expand downward into compassion."

Robert Bly

Western techno-monster culture has been as damaging to men as it has been to women. Everywhere on TV we see suited, neck-tied men speaking in false voices, selling cars. Why is it that we don't trust car salesmen? It's their voices. They never speak naturally. They are modulated to sell whether we want to buy or not. Suited, neck-tied men appear on the news. Talking heads speaking in smooth, even tones about murder, catastrophe, crime... no emotional inflection... objective facts... "150 people were killed as a plane crashed... thousands died in an earthquake... a priest is accused of pedophilia." Or we hear the practiced emotional appeal of the suited and neck-tied politicians promising and promising— if we will only vote them into office.

Where is the authentic male voice heard today? The voice full of a man's multi-dimensionality, not held by social constraints? The reality of a man's feelings, strivings, longings and dreams often goes unheard. Where is the deep inner power of a man's knowing, not the power to buy, power to deal, power over someone else. This hierarchical toe-the-line power suffocates men and women and prevents all of us from embracing our fullest human qualities. Conforming to the narrow parameters of this heirarchy diminishes the freedom of our inner life; it makes us doubt the voice of our soul.

Men struggle with many of the same voice issues as women. Men have been silenced in many of the same ways through physical, verbal and sexual abuse. Many men with naturally loud or exuberant voices were told to "tone down" and "blend in" or simply to "shut up." Men, too often, learned this message by not seeing other men express themselves emotionally. "I never saw my father cry," is a common statement I have heard from men.

When men remember their childhood experiences with singing a sense of shame often comes to the surface. Men have a unique life change occur as their voice dramatically changes in adolesence. Garrison Keillor has recounted, bittersweetly, that "rhythm is not our problem in the tenor section. We do drag a little bit. But notes are our problem. And the reason that we drag is that each one of us in the tenor section is waiting to hear the person next to him sing the note so we can get it. Each one of us is trying to sing a little softer than the boy next to him. Because, though we are tenors, we are in the last few months of our tenor voices and they are undependable."[1]

Sometimes men with beautiful boy soprano voices are asked to leave choir when their voices deepen. Or, if boys' voices don't deepen enough, they can become objects of ridicule. Many men who have taken my workshops have said they remember laughing at boys with high-pitched voices and remember being laughed at as well for their own voice. One man told me that he consciously lowers his voice when he is in groups of men or when he goes into a hardware store or talks with a mechanic.

There are subtle pressures that give the message that if you're a man you don't sing.

> A man remembers getting stared at by other men for singing enthusiastically in church.
>
> A man remembers not singing because he didn't think his voice was perfect.
>
> A man remembers his voice teacher, a male opera singer, trying to sexually molest him.
>
> A man says, "I don't hear men sing spontaneously."
>
> A man remembers a lot of joking when spontaneous singing emerged around a campfire with other men.
>
> A man remembers men cutting each other down with a joke when someone sings along to the radio. "Do you know why Paul Simon is singing that song? So you don't have to."
>
> A man remembers subtle cultural pressures around singing. "No one ever told me not to sing. But singing is not even in my mindset. There is no consideration for singing. It's not what people do. As a society we don't respect singers."
>
> A Dagwood cartoon shows Dagwood singing in the bathtub. A burly, male stranger walks in the door and shouts, "If you don't stop singing I'm going to shove this bar of soap down your throat!"
>
> An eight-year-old boy says, "Singing is for girls."

This background of subtle, or overt, cultural pressure takes its toll on men's willingness to sing. Yet many men do have wonderful memories of singing. And men who succeed at singing can become heroes, even if they don't have great voices.

> A man remembers his Bar Mitzvah and being mentored by a cantor so he could sing in front of the congregation. "This was the only part of the Bar Mitzvah that felt like an initiation. I became part of a mystery."
>
> A man remembers singing more with a male friend more than talking and says, "Singing is a great way to be with a man."
>
> A man remembers singing all the time with two other boys on a school bus in the midwest. They called themselves "The Cornfield Trio."
>
> A man remembers being an outcast until the Beatles became popular, he formed a rock band and sang. "I had been in Nerdsville before that and now I was cool. It felt good to sing. The one who sings is the one who gets to be the leader of a band."

Some singing experiences are uniquely male. Remember the singing cowboy? Around the campfires of the expanding western frontier cowboys would sing, sometimes with raised head, "howling out his song like the lobo wolf."[2] A different form of introduction awaited new cowboys, "When a puncher from another outfit drifted into camp, he was expected to sing any new song he might know or new stanzas to an old song, and to teach to the camp he was visiting."[3] Later we would hear of Gene Autrey, Roy Rogers, Bob Wills, Hank Williams— and then the billion dollar country western music industry.

Men's Voices

In the pueblos of the southwest it is the men who sing and drum at the ceremonial dances. For Tewa pueblos, the Cloud Dance is a song celebrating the seasons, the four directions, the colors of nature and the earth's goodness— and the singer himself is at the center of that cycle. For singer and teacher Peter Garcia, songs were simply part of life. "I heard my dad sing this one way back... My dad was a great composer of Indian songs." Now, as leader of the San Juan Indian Youth Dancers, he teaches them the old songs with the Buffalo, Eagle, Butterfly and Dog dances. Songs remain at the center of his world, just as they were at the heart of his father's. He has dedicated himself to creating his own songs and these songs have become part of the pueblo's dances with his own children and grandchildren dancing.[4]

Every man has a different experience with singing. The overall cultural context in which a man lives can either stifle or nurture his voice. In the following, the personal stories of several men will be heard: first from a group toning experience, then in interviews with three different men who regard themselves as singers.

- Six men between the ages of 40 and 60 met one summer's evening to participate in a group toning and a discussion on men's voices. These men comprise a diversity of backgrounds and professions. One is a therapist, one works in a prison system, one man is a contractor, another a painter, four are poets, one works for the city. I ask if any of them sing while in the shower. No one. Two sing in the car along with the radio sometimes. One sometimes sings in the car without the radio with other people. Two like the voices they have, the rest don't. No one sings every day. No one considers himself to be a singer. However, as we talk it becomes clear that each man has something to say about song, sometimes in very moving ways.

As we share turns talking, I ask each man to say something about his voice and singing:

1st man:

"I love to hear my voice and when I started to write poetry one of the first things I realized was that I needed to discover my voice. When I read poetry I find that voice and speak through it. It has a lot of feeling in it. My stuff goes back to old gospel hymns. I love that stuff. I refer to these songs as my angels. Singing has always been a part of my life. My wife's father is 96 years old. When we ride together in the car we all sing songs we know. He's so spirited by it. We're all uplifted by it. When I was a boy in church I used to sing all these songs like *'Heavenly Sunshine'* and I'd really go with it until someone told me I had to quiet down because I was getting too exuberant. I was really enthusiastic. After that I sat in church most of the time and caught flies."

2nd man:

"I remember when I was very young I sang. I don't know when I stopped. I feel very self-conscious about singing. When I sang after that it was in drinking bouts. We'd get to sing when we'd drink in Irish and Welsh taverns. That lifts you up. Now I work at a place where I'm alone sometimes in a building with great acoustics and I sing the blues. I can't think of one person in my family that I ever overheard singing. Ever. There just wasn't a setting for that."

3rd man:

"I don't have much of a singing voice. No one in my family sang either that I remember. I love to listen to opera and admire the voices. It leaves me with a feeling that I could never be like that. I'm surprised at myself for not singing in the shower. Seems to me I ought to be doing that. It seems to me to be a cliche in our society that men are supposed to sing in the shower. I don't know where I got that. Maybe from sitcoms or cartoons. Maybe I should start. At any rate I'm a non-singer."

4th man:

"This is bringing back all sorts of memories. I grew up Jewish. When I was in college my best friend moved in for several years as a roommate. His family was very church oriented and I went to church with them. I found out, 'Geez, you can sing out loud in church and nobody can hear you!' So every chance I got I had to go to church to sing the hymns. I'd go and help them out. It was the only place I could go to sing. When I was a kid I was told I had a lousy voice and couldn't carry a tune. Happened all the time in my last marriage. My wife and I would be in the car and my wife would say, 'Oh, God!' and make a choking motion when I sang. My step-daughter could carry a tune well, my youngest son could, too, and my wife had a very good voice. They couldn't stand to listen to me because I was always off key. I'm still very affected by this. Bobby McFerrin in concert is close to a religious experience. Now I'm a member of a spiritual group and in it we do exercises that express sounds. That's where all my singing happens."

5th man:

"I'm struck by what's been mentioned so far. I don't remember anyone in my family singing either. I went to a boys' school for a few years and they had a choir and a decent choir director. I sang in the choir for a short period of time. I don't feel I have a good singing voice. Part of the director's job was to get you to enunciate and sing the way he wanted you to sing. I was made to go to church as a kid and remember a lot of music and singing in church. Some of which becomes meaningful and important by virtue of the fact of hearing it so many times. Some of it I don't care for much. At Easter time you hear the same hymns and become saturated with them. When I started doing yoga the teacher did chanting with us and it was a very powerful group experience. The relaxation that took place beforehand seemed to give my intonation a different power that I could express for a longer period of time. It carried power in the whole group. You weren't doing it by yourself. The total was more than the sum of its parts. When someone would wane someone else in the group would be strong. In the group you lose your own self-consciousness about your own voice. There's something about the voice. Perhaps it carries your power or something. I feel like mine has been stifled for a long time and I don't know why."

6th man:

"I don't remember anyone in my family singing much at all. Except every Christmas when we had big family get-togethers my dad would get a bunch of the little kids together and sing *'Bye Bye Blackbird'* to them. I never paid attention at the time but I think it was after he had a few drinks in him. I remember being so embarrassed when he'd do that. My grandfather used to play spirituals by Tennessee Ernie Ford but I don't remember him ever singing along. That's the only thing I can remember about people being interested in music in my family.

When I was 9 or 10 a friend down the block gave me a pile of 78 records and I would love to listen to them and sometimes sing along. I was self-conscious singing in church but the music would affect me. I was always too self-conscious to go out for choir except in my senior year I did and got in. It was wonderful. I felt very proud I could do that.

I got more and more into popular music in college. When I sang my whole being was bigger. I'd sing and it would be an ecstatic release that was just incredible. I could do it alone. There was a period of about ten years or more when singing along with the music was the only thing that kept me in touch with my emotions at all. It was a safe place to sit and listen to music and sing. I could see how I felt and learn about myself.

When I got into therapy years later, people in my group always asked me to speak up. I was most inaudible when I was less sure of myself. Group therapy was the most comfortable place I'd ever been and I wanted someone to hear me sing, so I brought my tape recorder and tried singing to the group and it felt good to do that. Eventually I sang just about as freely and with as much intensity as I did alone. To do that with other people watching made a huge difference. It was very valuable. I very rarely have anyone ask me to speak up any more."

1st man:

"I can't shed tears very easily until I listen to music. There are certain records and music that I play when I want to shed tears. I'll feel this swelling effect in my chest and I can't quite let it go. It's like an armor. Music is the only thing I know that makes crying come easier. *'Ave Maria'* touches something so far down there it gets below my hurts."

This was the perfect place to introduce toning, since it concerns the ability to express one's self emotionally. I talked through the experience and then we began. Low groans and rumbles resounded throughout the room. How marvelous to hear these deep rich voices begin to emerge from within each man. Some of the tones sounded painful, some were chant-like exploration. In the silence afterwards, there was a different feeling in the room. Everyone felt more relaxed and in touch with what they were feeling. Many felt sensations in their bodies: energy coming off their hands and feet; resonance in the head and chest; several noticed tight jaws, tight stomachs and shallow breathing. These responses are common to any group beginning to tone.

The second toning was longer, louder, stronger and more resonant. It started low and rose in pitch and intensity. I wanted to withdraw my feminine voice and listen more clearly to each man's voice and the full range of strength and beauty I heard but, since this was still a new experience, I kept toning so I could support the unfolding with my own voice. Sometimes I stayed in the same tonal range and sometimes lifted my voice above as a counterpoint. The group commented they felt more resonance, freedom, experimentation and spontaneity. The man with the tight jaw said opening his mouth more was important to allowing himself to be expressive.

One man asked if this sounded any different than the women's toning groups I lead and I said I heard power being voiced immediately. I felt the two tonings resonating in my solar plexus area. I said women get to this place too, but it often takes awhile to feel comfortable hanging out in this terrain because of fears around power. I told them stories that women have told me about the fears against allowing themselves to feel power— a fear that they will use their strength abusively. Several men nodded and one man said he used to feel a lot of fear around abusing power too. Others remarked that too often men's voices are only used as weapons or to sell something.

Yet some men do sing. Some men really love to sing.

Forrest Evans is a friend of mine and I asked him about being a man and being a singer. Forrest sings with a contemporary Albuquerque band— *SaHa World Telegraph* .

Forrest told me his story:

> "I knew I had a Welsh background but I didn't pay any attention to it. I always sang. Everybody in my family sings. My parents sang in the church choir. We sang at home, my sisters sang, one sister studied classical singing and another sister wrote songs, my brother played bass and wrote songs. It was definitely an environment which nurtured singing. We were always singing. Later, when I found myself in New Mexico, I joined a Welsh choir. I sang with them for a couple of years and connected with those Welsh roots and found that the Welsh absolutely love to sing. The thing that Wales is most noted for is singing. And the most famous aspect of that is the male choirs of Wales. Last year a 100-voice male choir came to New Mexico and performed in Albuquerque. They were tremendous singers. I heard stories that when they really got to singing was after the concert. They went down to the Rio Grande Cantina and closed the place down. They drank all the beer the place had and sang songs until they were blue in the face. Then they went to some hotel and they closed that place down. They went into the lobby and sang in the lobby until 2 or 3 in the morning. They were finally kicked out.

"I often find myself in situations where people have never sung before and as an adult it has struck me as a peculiar aspect of our culture today. In this society there are so many perfect recordings on compact discs and tapes that people separate themselves into singers and musicians who are serious about it and people who are just listeners. My family came from a place in Maine where people gathered around the piano or organ and just sang together. Old traditional ways still existed and modern times hadn't robbed us of our heritage of not being afraid to sing together.

"I get very high when I sing. I just flow along with the river of sound. I'll feel the sound and get intoxicated by it. There is a place where I lose myself. Sometimes it gets in the way of being a serious professional singer because I get to a place where I don't want to work out all the details of how to sing well, learning how to enunciate and being precise about intonation.

"I've studied classical singing off and on for fourteen years. When I first started I was living in Santa Fe and studying with this woman who was trying to get me to have a big open sound. I didn't have a clue about how to be a classical singer but I was enjoying getting that sound. She would have me go out on a hill and sing to the next hill.

"The first time I did toning was with you at one of your *Circle the Earth with Song* gatherings. I hadn't toned before but I'd done some things that were similar. At Kent State I'd walk through the woods on the way to class. There were lots of birds and I'd emulate birds. I've always liked making funny sounds with my voice. Toning gave me more of a structure. It helped me further to touch the essential basis of singing. Toning is like the root which comes to the surface. Then you can shape it up at the top with technique or other choices you make. But the real deep emotional content is what comes up through the toning. I've thought of it like going back and forth between two worlds, the conscious and the unconscious. If I'm going to sing a song all written out I can approach it from a technical point of view and work on it but I can't get at the feeling until I do some toning. Then you come back to the song with something richer.

"I've led singing groups and used toning. I express myself freely so that freedom will be heard, I hope to encourage other people to be free themselves so they will feel the openness. People react very easily to that freedom. It's heartwarming to hear people let go of their stuff and come in contact with a freedom they haven't experienced before. I think it's very beautiful. Something in them recognizes the need to sing. I tell people that they use their voices every day to make sense and here's an opportunity where they don't have to make any sense.

"More women than men come to my groups. More women than men dance. I play in a band and when the music starts the first people to hit the dance floor are the women. What about the men? It's the same with singing. In American culture men have somehow tied themselves up into some kind of knots of what we think a man is supposed to be. Those knots are tied so tight it takes 3 or 4 beers to get them loose. Typically in bars men will dance and sing too. Men will get drunk and then they'll sing. That's showing that the psychological bonds are very tight. What's happened in this culture to make this happen? We're not a primal culture. We're not in touch with our bodies. We're not in touch with the seasons. We're just not in touch. We're a very intellectual society and the rational mind says that it's not cool to sing. It's true more for white American culture. You look at the black culture and it's not a problem at all.

My maturing as a person has had a lot to do directly with changes that have happened in my singing. I open up and sing and I'm not afraid. I've done meditation retreats where you don't make any sounds at all and you come all the way to the root of silence. You come to the roots of who you are and why you would even bother to sing in the first place. Those kinds of things are important in making a free sound.

Singing is a joyful thing. It's an expression of our joy at having our bodies and being in this form. I maybe come from a formless void somewhere where there are no bodies, no voices, no women and no men and now I have a voice and I am a man and it's healing and joyful. Singing is the expression of the glory of creation, the mystery of it all, sometimes the sadness of it all. To express this through the voice is very powerful.

At the end of a meditation retreat I attended, they had this piano and I went up to it and played one note after a week of silence and it made me cry. What one sound can mean and be. One note you sing is so powerful and mysterious it shakes the earth. It's really about one note, one moment, if you really let yourself sink into it. If you go down deep you'll find whatever it is you are."

When I arrived to interview John Stokes, singer, musician, storyteller and director of *The Tracking Project,* I was met by a father saying goodbye to his 2 ½-year-old daughter. His goodbye was like a song. "I like to rap-ify everything with her," he told me later. He took me inside his office and the first thing he asked me was "Have you ever seen a hummingbird's nest?" He showed me a delicate but strong work of art. He talked about singing to the squirrels and other animals which come by his office in the rural community of Corrales, New Mexico. He was getting ready to take a group of teenage boys out for a week: The HawkEye Training. He talked about the importance of being an uncle to them and the importance of men being uncles to each other.

I asked him about his involvement with the Men's Gatherings where he joined Robert Bly, James Hillman and Michael Meade in different places around the country for five years. He pointed to a huge cloth painting of the Virgin Mary.

> "That's who had me go to the men's conferences, right there. I was sitting in a chair over there and the phone rang and that fell off the wall and wrapped around me. I thought 'Well, this is going to be an interesting call!' and it was my old friend Robert Bly who I'd known since I worked at the Beacon Press. He invited me to be a part of the conference. I hung up the phone and said, 'I don't want to spend a week with 100 men,' and she said, 'Yes, you do.' So I went there and sat up in front. I was thinking I was supposed to be this strong male teacher and there were just tears rolling down my cheeks. I stood up and said, 'I'm not crying for any of you. I'm crying for us all. I haven't been in a room full of white men ever in my life. I've always been with native guys. I just spent the last seven years with all black men being the only white face in this room filled with black men. I never heard them complain about any of the things I'm hearing today. I'm so sorry we've lived this way and

have to discuss these things.' I'm kind of contrary that way. My maleness had come from a completely other place, from a matrilineal initiatory cycle. I really learned a lot about us at these men's conferences. I tried to bring the voice of nature and the voice of music to them.

"I'm Welsh and Turkish, 50% of each. From the Welsh I got the singing. I sang for a lot of my life and guys would say, 'C'mon John, give it a rest.' Just guys hearing you sing. But the women would say, 'No, sing. That's good. Your voice is good!' They'd encourage me. I eventually got a job as a country western guitar player in an Aboriginal Community College back in 1977. I started to sing and they would all drop everything and come and sit and listen. They said my voice had a certain quality that was very beautiful. They said, 'You're the kind that could make the birds all come and land on your shoulders.' I was contrasting this with what I heard all the rest of my life and I thought maybe they were making fun of me. This was in Adelaide, South Australia. I thought I was being led on, but I went ahead and sang. My music classes started to grow. I began to use my music and I was introduced to the didjeridu. The didjeridu is really a tube that can take the human voice and extend it into other realms way beyond what I've ever heard someone do with just their voice. The didjeridu is now a well known instrument. At the time it wasn't well known at all. It was exclusively a male instrument. There are certain things that are allowed to men by the women of native cultures. One because the men need it, and two, because men have to do certain things through ceremony that women can do with their bodies. One of those things is to fertilize the world.

"In the Aboriginal world (and I'm making a generalization about a whole continent, which is dicey) the women control this material world. It's not for men to mess around with this world, it's not our business. Men's business is with the spiritual world. Men deal with the world of the unborn and the world of the dead. The unborn and the dead are both in the same place and they come out of the vastness and they strive to be born. Once they are born into this world the women care for those things. Then they die and go back to the spirit land, that clan pool. The men deal with that world. That's why men are always out fasting and dreaming and doing their ceremonies so they can stay in touch with that spiritual world. This is the Aboriginal concept.

"The didjeridu is used to fertilize the world with song and to increase the fertility of the species. To touch it is so potentially sexual that the old admonition was that a woman would become pregnant just to hold the didjeridu. It's just a long hollow tube. They also explained to me that, like all Aboriginal things, nothing is completely male or completely female. If you look at it one way as a long tube you can see that it's a man. But if you look at it through the tube you can see that it's a female that represents all the things in our world that are whole.

"The old men heard me singing and they saw that I was 'out there' and they kept pulling me aside and sitting me in the corner and playing the didjeridu with me. They were filling me with magical words. You make the sound with circular breathing. The tribal people I worked with talk that way. So they talk on the outbreath and they talk on the inbreath and they don't ever stop. They just talk in this long way. So, my instruction was taking place on my lunch hour. It was like another dimension. We'd sit in the corner and play. You blow the didjeridu into the corner so you can hear the sound come back to you. It's so resonant it makes your head vibrate. You can't truly hear what you play. I learned to play the didjeridu and a million things came from that, from having whales dance to it, to calling the birds out of the sky. It's a very magical instrument. My knowledge of singing and men's business and all that came from playing the didjeridu.

"I was coming from this place when I got back here to America. I was saddened when I saw how we had lost magic. I personally feel we're not going to think our way out of this. We could sing our way out of this. We could laugh our way out. We could pray out way out but we're not going to think our way out.

"I was with Gary Snyder the poet. I set up a tour for him in Australia. As we drove to Nimbin to meet with John Seed, the man who works with the rain forest, I was singing Bob Marley songs a capella in the car to pass time during the long drive. Gary Snyder had never listened to the words. He kept egging me on. For the rest of the tour Gary would introduce me and he'd say, 'This is John Stokes. He's a singer.' No one had ever said that to me before. It was remarkable. It was beautiful to be introduced that way. There's a scene in the beginning of the movie *MEETINGS WITH REMARKABLE MEN* where they have a music contest. The man who can stand up and sing and make the mountain vibrate is the winner. He gets a lamb. That man had a red beard and I did too. I identified with that. When Gary Snyder, who was quite a hero of mine, introduced me as a singer it was quite a blessing for a young man.

"I got away from singing for awhile after I left the *Tom Brown Jr. Tracking School* and started a business of my own. There I was teaching music, singing, storytelling and dancing as survival tools. The spirit cannot survive without those things. You can survive at the top of the hill with your gun and your camouflage but that sort of mountain man mentality isn't survival at all. So I was introducing music and tribal rhythm into this survival school. Let's start the day singing, start the day with poetry. I left the tracking school where I was doing that regularly. I had to establish a business. I lost the rhythm. I had to get into more of a modern rhythm which doesn't require singing at all. You listen to someone else do it for you.

"I got away from singing but got back to it when I met a Hawaiian man named Parley. It was just beautiful. He heard my voice speaking and asked me to chant and tone and he really liked it. He taught me some old songs and chants. I chant now and play the didjeridu and have all these tools to express my voice.

"The singing helps me to be what I am. I begin every day with a chant that I was given by Parley. I sit quietly, think, pray and chant for about an hour every morning. I sing to the sun and to the first animal that I meet. I sing with my daughter. We make up songs. It's incredible how much you can learn if you sing and make music every day. I'm astounded by the parts of the brain we can access when we enter into singing. Where I go when I really sing is what the Aborigines would call the Creative time, the beginning of time. There are many stories of the Rainbow serpent or some great hero who went to the sites where the energy was lodged in the earth and he sang the seed syllable that would unlock that energy.

"The magic of the things I learned in the tribal world were about using your intent, speaking clearly, letting your voice move things. I heard and I believe in the stories of people who grew plants to maturity in a day or two using their voice and music, moving large objects with your voice, using your voice to call animals. I've been with men who could do that and I've seen them do it. I've seen animals that everyone is terrified of called by men standing there calling the name of that animal, a specific member of that species, not just any animal. Having seen that and knowing it's within the realm of human possibility I'm not afraid to try it.

"When I work with men in nature I don't want to know about all the troubles they have. I say, 'C'mon, let's go outside and remember what it was like to be the first man.' We go out and through breathing and movement we begin. We go through some words of condolence. I know they're feeling grief. Should I ask, 'Are you guys feeling some grief?' No, just do the condolences.

"The Iroquois have words that they share with somebody who's lost a loved one. My friend Jake Swamp believes that grief and denial are all connected. Nobody can hear, nobody can listen, nobody can sing, nobody can see because we're all exhibiting the symptoms of deep grief.

When you're in grief you cry. You can't see any more, so they have a way to wipe away the tears with a fawnskin taken from the sky. When you cry so much the sobs lodge in your ears, what they call the dust of death, so you wipe the dust from the ears with a feather taken from the sky so you can hear the birds again. Then you give them water from the Creator and help them wash the lump of grief from their throat because food won't go down and water can't go down and they can't speak or sing.

The condolences go on and on and on describing the symptoms of grief. There are 13 of them. We do for of these for people. That's how we begin our gatherings.

"Condolences are spoken. But when you hear most of the old languages they're very techni-colored, they're three dimensional CD-Rom utterances and they don't have much to do with the way we speak. We open with three whoops that announce to the spirit that you're about to do something important. That's what we do. We're getting ready to do this with a group of 12 to 18-year-old boys at a week-long skills camp. Boys come from all over the country. We do it like that all day and the kids come back jamming."

When I hear these stories from men I am struck by their desire to sing and the personal freedom that singing brings. How the voice flourishes with permission and nurturing! I think of ways in which men have been initiated as singers... the Bar Mitzvah, the Pueblo dances, the blessing from a hero and how important it is that male voices are heard. I welcome a world where men, women and children listen to each other sing— and support each other's authentic expression through tone and song.

This vision is coming to reality in many different places throughout the world. One place is Joesph Rael's sound chamber in New Mexico. Joseph is a visionary, teacher, and author from Tiwa and Ute heritage. He grew up on Picuris Pueblo in Northern New Mexico and has studied sound and language all his life. He speaks his native Tiwa, Spanish and English fluently.

Joseph Rael, *Beautiful Painted Arrow*, was waiting outside his gate as I drove up. He had just returned from leading a Long Dance in Boulder, Colorado and was getting ready to lead another in New Mexico. Ten years ago, Joseph had a vision to build a Sound Chamber where people could chant for peace. In a second vision, he saw a ring of light descend next to his home in Bernalillo, New Mexico and he built the first Sound Chamber there. Today, ten years later, there are twenty five Sound Chambers all over the world. I had been in his Sound Chamber over the years, but most recently attended the tenth anniversary of his vision held January 1, 1994.

Joseph joined me in the Sound Chamber and began to talk about sound and silence:

> "Silence gives you the key to what becomes audible. Silence is what purifies what becomes audible. Through singing the here and now is created. If everyone should stop singing, vibration would stop from the place of silence and we would basically disappear. Though the original, principle ideas would still be what they are, since their essence always was and always exists. In this dimension, we're looking at the crystallization of ideas. Sound is the one that creates the here and now because everything is singing to God. Silence is what gives sound its foundation. Without silence there would be no foundation for sound, it would just fall and fall and fall and have no place to land. Silence gives sound a place to stand.
>
> "Sound is the beauty that is connected to all heavenly planes. It has a very high clarity that washes everything. It's a connector to how we can know who we are personally. It crystallizes everything so we can see it, touch it, grab it, taste it. It fills us with goodness. Chanting sounds becomes a way of joy."

Joseph begins to talk about language. In his study of different languages he began to notice root sounds in all of them. Studying and reflecting on these sounds led him to the mysteries of their meanings. These sounds form the foundation of his chanting:

"Aah" (the A sound in Spanish) — Purification, direction of the east, mental body
"Eh" (the E sound in Spanish) — Relationship, direction of the south, emotional body
"Eee" (the I sound in Spanish) — Awareness, direction of the west, physical body
"Oh" (the O sound in Spanish) — Innocence, the Infinite Void, direction of the north, spiritual body
"Uu" (the U sound in Spanish) — Carrying, center of the medicine wheel[5]

Joseph believes, "We are creating what's happening on the planet by our thoughts and how we speak the language that we speak. We create the socio-economic-political systems. We have different systems such as capitalism. All these systems are perpetuated by the languages that we speak. So we have to go back to language to find out how we are living our lives and go back to discover how it is we can change things.

"Everything comes from the land. The original languages came from the land. The original ideas came from the land. People were learning from the land, original languages they wanted to speak so they could stay close to God. To be an inch away from original vibration could be seen as a very vulnerable place. That's how languages began. The very nature of technology calls for separation because technology is intended to manipulate the environment. Manipulation is the first step towards separation. Some people would say it's the first step towards evil. You're changing something to meet the needs of the situation perhaps at the very expense of ecology. All languages have these five basic sounds. Sound is sound. Whether you know it or not you're contributing, either consciously or unconsciously to what's going on on the planet."

In the Sound Chambers, men and women chant together for peace and harmony. Joseph received a planetary vision so powerful that it inspired him to create these chambers around the world.

> *"Before me is standing a man who is made of light and his whole body is singing. The man becomes an oval chamber and I see women and men singing in it. And I am told that they chant for peace. The vision lasted three seconds, yet I saw in moments—years of world peace.*

"In my vision Man was the symbol of light that was emanating from the Infinite Self and that is what I saw. The oval-shaped chamber was the symbol of the beginning of life. Therefore, the Being of Chanting and the Being of Vision were telling me that when we chant in ceremony we go back to the beginning before we became the six passions. These passions are greed, pride, attachment, mental obscuration, jealousy, and anger. Through chanting we realize that we can personally affect and change the vibrations we acquired after life first began.

"The Chamber helps us individually transcend personal identity so that we may enter the Greater Reality and our connectedness to all things. This resonant wave thus becomes an energy base with which to bring peace and healing of the Earth into manifestation."[6]

In order for peace to exist, men's and women's voices chanting together are needed. "According to the ancients, the extension of the feminine is the masculine, another way of stating this is that which descends is female and when it lands on the floor it becomes male. So in chanting, both feminine and masculine energies are involved. The feminine brings down from the higher mind the sustenance of sound and the male then expresses sound."[7]

This principle is expressed in the ceremonial life of the Tiwa people. In dances at the pueblos open to the public, the men are the singers. "The unfolding of the feminine is the masculine— so who's singing? Not the men, you're seeing men's bodies. The ceremonies might have gone on for 6 to 8 weeks in the kivas and women are involved there singing. But when they come out in the open it will be the men singing, because at that point it's the unfolding of the feminine through the masculine so you don't see the women singing. Women sing in the chambers which is made from the sound. It's not until it comes out of the ground into the light that it is the expression of the masculine. The land is infinity, infinity is the breath, the breath is dark so you have the dark chambers. The feminine, in here, in the chambers, starts it, but as soon as it comes out into the light that's the masculine. The unfolding of the feminine is the masculine. The feminine creates it and the masculine expresses it."[8]

Joseph sees this relationship between the masculine and the feminine as we breathe and chant. "The inhalation is the metaphor of Father Sky and the exhalation represents Mother Earth.

We seek to keep earth and sky and ourselves bonded together and enhance them through chanting. When we chant, we are giving energy to their connection. Historically speaking, separation has led to world unrest, wars, etc. and at a personal level, we feel disconnected because of the lack of connection between earth, sky and ourselves. The theory is that as we chant our physical bodies into finer attunement, the people living on the earth and the living earth itself will find peace."[9]

Opening quote: Robert Bly, James Hillman and Michael Meade, *The Rag and Bone Shop of the Heart: Poems for Men,* Harper Perennial, New York, 1992, p. 97-98.

1. Garrison Keillor, audiotape "The Seasons, Spring", Minnesota Public Radio.
2. John A. and Alan Lomax (ed.), *Cowboy songs and Other Frontier Ballads,* Macmillan Publishing Co., New York, 1986, p. xix
3. Ibid.
4. Jim Sagel, "New Songs, Young Feet Carry On Ancient Messages", Albuquerque Journal, Feb. 25, 1987.
5. Joseph Rael with Mary Elizabeth Marlow, *Being and Vibration*, Council Oak Books, Tulsa, Oklahoma, 1993, pp. 125-126.
6. Joseph Rael, *Peace Chambers* brochure, self-published, Bernalillo, New Mexico, n.d.
7. *Being and Vibration*, p. 120
8. Personal interview with Joseph Rael.
9. Rael and Marlow, *Being and Vibration*, p. 128.

Verse III

Earth Voices

"Until morning they sing songs of rain and cloud,
of little red spiders and the little gray horned toads
who are the friends of the rain,
and of the frogs who are its messengers."
Ruth Murray Underhill

All over the world people sing praises to the beauty of the earth. For every season, songs are born out of the human heart. People sing to bring up the sun and raise up the moon. Zunis in New Mexico sing the sun awake at dawn with— "We are grateful for another day."[1]

After awakening, Australian Aborigines go alone into the bush to create songs based on nightly dreams. They believe the animals and birds "hear the dreams being sung and recognize the singer is in touch with the inner world, and therefore assist him or her in daily hunting and gathering."[2]

Each place on earth has a different vibrational pattern and the languages, sounds and music are reflections of a more intimate listening to that place. We've forgotten how this has happened.

Language and music pass down without people thinking of their origin. The earth in New Mexico sounds different than the earth in Colorado and either sounds different than the Pacific Northwest. Even though there are sounds common to all places, they combine in particular ways in unique frequencies. Vibrational patterns are integrated within an ecology, each place has its own way of speaking. One of my goals is to try and listen to this language and, perhaps, engage in conversation.

In recent times, due to the growing global problems with our environment, many groups throughout the world sing chants in honor of the earth— "The earth is our mother, we must take care of her, her sacred ground we walk upon with every step we take."

In 1986 when I recorded my cassette *"Circle the Earth with Song"* I didn't realize it would literally circle the earth. The tape was recorded on a shoe-string budget with the support of friends. I sent out several announcements to the newsletters of national organizations to which I belonged. I gave demo copies to bookstores in whatever state I was visiting. A favorable review appeared in *Heartsong Review.* In the first year I was getting orders from people I didn't know, in countries I had never visited. People from all over the United States, Canada, New Zealand, Australia, England, Germany, France, and Africa ordered the tape. People from all over the world listened to the tape and sang along with it. Somehow because of my intention to *"Circle the Earth with Song"* the tape grew wings and began to have a life of its own. For the liner notes I wrote:

> "The chants on this tape are simple and repetitive. They are seeds with which to create your own verses, harmonies or songs. They are presented so that you may find your own voice and your own songs.

"These chants were learned at workshops and gatherings throughout the country. Some were created spontaneously in response to inner images and feelings. Others were handed down from group to group, their origins lost like the anonymous folk songs of our ancestors. With each new singing, inevitable changes occur as the memory plays tricks with melody or text, creating different versions of the same song. For example, in Baltimore I learned a song from The Ghost Dance of the Plains Indians:

We circle around
We circle around
The boundaries of the earth
Wearing our long tail feathers as we fly
Higher, higher, higher

"In Kansas, I learned a different tune with the words 'higher, higher, higher' omitted. In California they wore 'long green feathers.' In England, it was 'long wing feathers.' Though minor changes occurred, the spirit of the song remained the same. This chant has literally circled the earth, creating a vibrational network, linked by the song's inner myth.

"These chants are part of the living mythology of which the earth, Gaia, is a central symbol. 'The earth is our mother, we must take care of her,' is the message inherent in the mythology of our times. We are at the point of crisis because, as a western technological culture, we have abused the earth. It has always been at times of crisis that new myths arise and are enacted through ritual to create order and harmony.

Chanting has always been an essential element of ritual, carrying the message and emotion of the myth. The songs we sing and the changes we make in our daily lives form our history."[3]

If the earth was created by song, as ancient voices attest to, then perhaps song is needed to maintain the harmony of the earth. Every second, some form of degradation happens to this planet. There are many reasons for this, but one may be the basic fact that people do not honor the earth with song. Our culture has become separated, cut off from any sort of dialogue. Sometimes I wonder if singing itself hasn't become an endangered species. Or have we simply stopped listening and no longer know when the earth is speaking to us. And we have no reply.

These questions led me to the following story:

THE MAGIC POND

Once there was a magic pond high on a mountain top. The water in the pond was pure music. Ripples of sound and iridescent colors moved through the pond and healed all who came near enough to hear. The sound and color were the same.

A small green frog was the keeper of the pond. This frog had golden eyes and smooth green skin the color of spring leaves. She kept the pond renewed with song. She sang of the colors of dawn and her song reflected in the pond. She sang of the spiraling light of the stars and her song reflected in the pond. She sang of the full moon rising from the mountaintop and her song reflected in the pond. Her singing reflected the colors of the sky. And there in the pond the sun, moon and stars blended into iridescent music.

Earth Voices

Each day more of the sky's light was blended into the water. Each day the frog sang of heaven's harmony and this harmony came to earth as the colored water. Many came from far away. Many green growing things — flowers, birds, and animals — all creatures of the earth came to the shores of the pond so that they could hear the waters sing. Sometimes they would hear the frog sing. This was a special blessing.

All who came to the waters of this magic pond were renewed and refreshed. And when they went back to their everyday world, they took a little bit of the pond's magic with them through their voices. It was said that whoever drank of these waters would find their true voice. As singers came back from the pond, they sang of its harmony. And in this way the earth kept renewing itself. Plants, animals, birds, insects, reptiles and people all sang together in harmony. In this way life went on.

For centuries the frog sang the music down from the sky and blended it into the pond. For centuries many came for renewal and took music back to the four corners of the earth. Slowly this began to change. As the peoples of the earth began to grow from small villages to cities, many forgot to go to the pond. Only those living close to the earth remembered.

The cities grew and spread concrete over the earth. And as the concrete spread the people forgot the colorful music of the magic pond. As each day went by, more trees were destroyed. Other ponds were plowed over. More plants were uprooted. Everywhere this happened the color was replaced by the grey of concrete. The music was replaced by the sounds of machines. The iridescent music was forgotten. People forgot to sing. They forgot to dream.

The frog began to know this. She saw it in the eyes of those coming to the pond. She read it in the faces of those coming to be renewed. She felt it in the air. Even though everything near the pond was shimmering music, she knew that slowly, in the rest of the world, the old music was dying with the trees. She knew that in time the creatures of the earth would forget about the pond. For it was the trees whispering to each other in the breeze that told the story of the pond to all who were listening. Soon she knew, there would be no true listening as the sounds of the machines deadened the ears of the earth.

It became as she feared. Fewer and fewer came to the pond. First the people forgot to come. Then the animals forgot. The flowers forgot. The birds and insects forgot. All the creatures of the earth forgot. Soon she was the only singer left on the earth who sang of starlight weaving silver on the water or who sang of dawn blending gold in the waves. She could not go out to the great world to renew it as she could not live without the pond. The pond could not live without her. And the earth could not live without this music. She knew that the only hope she had was dreamsong.

Every night when the earth was asleep, she wove her song into the night as dreams. She sang of the pond, of the healing colors of rainbow sounds. All creatures of the earth heard her song in their dreams. All except the people. The creatures could not make the people listen to them or their dreams. As night came the frog sang again. She sang of the moon glowing like a pearl on the pond. Some of the people heard this dreamsong. But in the morning they forgot or only half-remembered as they rushed to work. Each night the frog sang. Sometimes little bits of the dreamsong were remembered. But since no one spoke of dreams anymore the dreamsong was not believed to be important. Night after night the frog sang her dreamsong. Day after day the people forgot.

The trees near the pond began to wither and the frog knew the machines were getting close. Soon the pond began to grow smaller. She knew that unless someone heard her dreamsong she and the pond would die. She paused in her song to listen to the sky. She listened to the sun and the moon, she listened to the stars, and she listened to the light. She breathed in the light and sang the sweetest song she had ever sung. She sang of the galaxies spinning through the night. She sang of comets chasing the stars. She sang the order of the heavens and she wove this music into her dreamsong. She sent this song out now, not to all the people of the world, but to only one. For she knew that if only one heard this dreamsong and sang it to the world it would be enough.

That night a young woman named Rose had a dream. It was the most beautiful dream she had ever dreamed. But it was also the most frightening. She heard an exquisite song sung by a tiny green frog with golden eyes. The frog sang a song of opalescent light glimmering on a pond. It was as if she could taste the water. It tasted like a nectar made of flowers, dew and starlight. As she drank the nectar, she felt every cell in her body awaken.

As she awakened, she saw what was happening around her. When was the last time she saw the stars? When was the last time she heard the trees whisper? She saw machines and concrete. Concrete and machines. Straight lines where there had once been groves of trees. Straight lines where there had once been circles of flowers. Through all this nightmare, she heard the little frog singing, singing of stars dancing on water.

In the morning her alarm went off and the dream tumbled around her. She rushed to get dressed and drove to work. But as she drove, she began to feel very sad. Where were the trees? She saw rows and rows of telephone poles. Where were the streams? There were straight canals lined with cement with dirty water flowing in them. Where were the animals? When was the last time she had seen a hawk? She began to cry.

In the middle of traffic, she stopped by a small tree growing by the side of the road. She remembered the dreamsong. Through her tears she began to sing. First she sang of what she saw around her

— the grey, the hardness of the concrete, the sounds of machines. People stopped their cars. Who was this woman wailing in the street? She must be crazy. They got out of their cars and moved towards her.

Her song changed. She sang of what had once been in this place — the trees, the plants, the gentle curve of the hills. She sang of springtime, of new leaves unfurling from buds, of blossoms and bees. She sang of moonlight glistening on water. She sang of a multi-colored pond with a green frog guardian who wove light into the water. Her song was like an elixir. The people realized how thirsty they were for this song. And as they drank of her music they began to sing. The tree by the road began to bloom, even though it was Fall. Birds returned to the sky. Streams broke through the concrete banks and flowed gracefully over the earth, carrying the song to the four corners of the earth.

The streams flowed to the place where the four corners converged. And there in the center was the magic pond and a tiny green frog singing with tears of joy. The pond grew until it was overflowing with song. Once again all the peoples of the earth, and all the creatures of the earth came to the pond. But instead of coming to the pond for healing, they brought healing to the pond. They sang of the earth and her seasons. They sang of trees growing tall. They sang of flowers blooming in meadows. They sang down the light from the heavens. They sang together in a harmony not heard upon this earth since she was new. The song reached up and touched the heavens, until it touched the stars themselves. The song was so beautiful that a great hush fell over the earth because everyone wanted to listen.

Out of the silence two voices were heard. A green frog sang in a clear voice bringing the gratitude of the starlight down from the sky. And a young woman named Rose sang the gratitude of the earth up to the sky. Their voices blended together and created a gentle rain. The rain was fragrant with stars and blossoms. As it fell upon the earth it washed away all that was grey until the earth was once again fresh and new.

Then something happened. Something which the stars had not heard in a long, long time. The earth began to sing. In a voice beyond ears, yet heard by all who would listen. She sang of the granite rocks high on the mountains. She sang of the fire within her core. She sang of the thin green cloak she wore decorated with flowering plants. And as she sang she brought a great light into herself. The stars welcomed her light into the vast night. All the people sang along and the earth was the brightest light in the sky. Tonight as you go to sleep, listen. She is singing now. Listen. Let her voice carry you into dreamsong. Wake to a new day singing.

What shape is the magic pond in today? Can we begin to find ways to join with ancient voices in singing to help restore the earth's beauty and balance?

One night I had a dream I was told to sing the forest. I live right next to a forest of juniper, alligator juniper, piñon, and pine. Were these trees singing to me? I had read about sounds from nature before. "David Cahen of the Weizman Institute of Science in Rehovot, Israel, and Gordon Kirkbright of the Imperial College in London have investigated the potential of photo-acoustic spectroscopy with particular care. Their work, called 'listening to the cells', has shown that even a simple corn stalk has a sound. Imagine thousands of stalks growing next to each other in a field, each with its own sound, a waving symphony of sounds. Certainly no human ear can hear it; and yet the symphony would not exist if there were no sensory system perceiving it."[4]

From years of refining my ability to listen, I noticed I was "hearing" something when I was alone in nature. It wasn't something I was hearing with my outer ears but something I knew with an inner ear. I was feeling and responding to the vibrations of nature. If corn stalks emit sounds then the possibility exists for all living things to emit sounds, even when we can't hear them with our physical human ears.

Forests can sing and we can sing with them. From this dream, and the growing perception that accompanied it, I developed the *Sing for the Earth* workshops as a way for people to have time alone in nature, to listen and create from what they hear.

The workshops take place in beautiful natural settings to help people attune to the world and themselves in new ways. When we listen to the earth we are given an opportunity to hear what the earth needs for her healing. We are given an opportunity to heal our personal relationship with the earth. Within the embrace of nature we can often free up blocks to our creativity.

As part of the workshop we honor the four directions: east, south, west and north. The directions have been invoked by peoples throughout the world as a way to create sacred space and to find one's connection to a deeper meaning of life. Each culture has variations on the meaning of each direction. In general, the directions follow daily and seasonal cycles:

> In the East the sun rises giving birth to a new day, light spreads over the face of the earth. The East is the place of new beginnings, of green shoots rising in the spring, of animals being born. During the spring birds return, hawks and eagles fly high. Whenever a fresh view is needed the spirits of the East are called to help.
>
> As the sun climbs high in the sky the direction of the South comes into full power. This is the summer of abundant growth, when flowers bloom in meadows. It is the time for

youthful play and innocence. Whenever these qualities are needed the spirits of the South are called to bring us back to trust.

When the sun sets on the horizon in the West we begin to go inward. It is the autumn of life, a time of harvest and a time to let go of what is no longer productive. This is the cycle of mid-life when we review what we have lost and what we have gained. The spirits of the West are called when we need to reflect on what life has given us.

At midnight, darkness and starlight fill the sky and we come to the direction of the North. Winter spreads a white coat over the earth, and, if we listen, the elders come to share their wisdom. All the doing of youth and middle age is replaced by Being. We call upon the spirits of the North whenever we need to sit quietly and listen for guidance.

Listening closely to which direction calls can help guide people in their own cyclic development and orient them in new ways. The following section describes two different *Sing for the Earth* workshops, one near my home in the Sandia Mountains of New Mexico and the other in Arizona's Superstition Mountains.

SING FOR THE EARTH

We sat inside a circle, four of us, one for each direction. As we passed a talking staff, we each spoke of our love and concern for the earth… concern for wild animals… love for the senses and physical delight of the body walking upon the earth. Concern for roads and development tearing up the land. Love for camping and offering cornmeal to the earth. Concern for the redwoods and the enormity of the devastation of natural places. Love of plants and herbs growing from the earth. Concern for cities spreading over the earth. Love for the beauty and the life the earth brings. All four of us were hearing the call to connect our work with the earth more, and to spend less time working indoors and more time outdoors.

We toned our love and concern for the earth. First there's a wailing sound for our concerns that grows softer with our love. We sing and honor the four directions, the four elements inside ourselves. We begin to feel power through our voices and intentions, power to heal our relationship with the earth.

Earth my body
Water my blood
Air my breath and
Fire my spirit[5]

(My body is of the earth. The earth's body supports and sustains me. The earth gives nourishment and peace. Earth my body... let me feel the earth of my body. Let us remember the simple ways of the earth.)

We sang:

We are alive as the earth is alive
We have the power to create our freedom
If we have courage we shall be healers
Like the sun we shall rise
If we have courage we shall be healers
Like the sun we shall rise[6]

We sing and acknowledge that today we come as healers. We are committed to the earth and to her greater healing. As we sing we hear the call of the forest outside. Birds begin to sing. Wind blows through the tree branches.

In many books on color therapy the color green is associated with healing. I ask the group to imagine breathing in green light to send to our bodies and through our hands, sending green light to the cornmeal bundles in the center of the circle which have been soaking up our intentions, our concern, our love, our song. We smudge the bundles with sage.

Outside we hike up the red rock trail to the pine grove on Sandia Mountain. The air is fragrant. We take long, full breathes and look out at the far view of the mountaintop, the distant trees. We look up at the turquoise New Mexico sky and to the sunlight in the pines. We look down at the red earth with its carpet of fallen pine needles. And as we turn and look in many directions we begin to sense what direction is calling to us today. We each take a short walk in that direction, not far from the circle. We walk and listen to the earth, how she is calling us. As we gather again I chant a Tewa Pueblo Prayer.

O our Mother the Earth
O our Father the Sky
Your children are we
And with tired backs
We bring you gifts of love
Then weave for us a garment of brightness
May the warp be the white light of morning
May the weft be the red light of evening
May the fringes be the falling rain

May the border be the standing rainbow
Then weave for us a garment of brightness
That we may walk fittingly where birds sing
That we may walk fittingly where grass is green
O our Mother the Earth
O our Father the Sky
Your children are we[7]

We dance and sing, drumming our footsteps into the earth, feeling our heartbeats beating with the heartbeat of the earth, feeling the pulsing of life move through us.

Then I sang my song for the earth, my song of the moment, singing the high pulsations of sunlight shining on pine needles, singing of the air and the slower pulses of the earth. When my song ended I spoke of these pulsations, of how each living thing has a pattern of vibration. The earth is always singing to us but our ears are often numbed by the sounds of civilization. What's it like not to be heard? Can we remember those times when we spoke and weren't listened to? How poignant those times are. How poignant it must be for the earth to continue to send out, every day, every moment, songs of beauty, offerings of sunsets and flowers and not be heard. We're too busy to stop and listen.

Listen. Listen to what is around you. Sing your response to the earth. Breathe into whatever you feel for the earth in this moment and send it forth in song.

We honored the silence after the toning. I asked if this toning was different than the toning they were all used to in *The Joy of Singing* class, or the toning inside a room, a shower, a car. Each woman spoke of the difference.

One felt more open inside. She sang in response to the tree in back of her and felt the vibrations of her voice connecting her with the tree. For another there was a moment of self-consciousness. Though she had toned before, this was new. How do you sing the wind? She gradually allowed herself to stop thinking about how to do this and allowed the wind song to move through her.

For another it was a singing of everything, of allowing all of the nature around her to sing through her, the trees, the mountain, the rocks, the clouds, the wind. She noticed more variety in her voice.

I then asked each woman to walk in the direction that called to her. They were asked to find a special place in this direction and in the center of this place to make an earth mandala out of the rocks, twigs, and pine cones that they found in this place. They were asked to offer cornmeal to this mandala. Then they sat and listened for a song or a poem. I told them to sing to this sacred place on the earth. When you hear the frog ocharina, a clay whistle I'll be playing, it's time to find your way back to the center in the pine grove where we began.

I walked slowly to the east, listening for a place that called to me. There on the ground before me were a multitude of flicker (woodpecker) feathers, bright orange spines of flicker feathers. A flicker must have been killed here by some other forest creature and its feathers fell on this very place. There on the forest floor was a nest of soft downy grey feathers as well as the bright orange feathers, and some larger black and white feathers. Some of these feathers had dots. Some were wisps blowing delicately in the wind. The universe had opened up in this moment. I felt profoundly blessed by this gift from the earth. I made my mandala around the central grey feathers. The central feather had a prominent black dot. The orange feathers were placed at the four directions. A circle of small pine cones and red rocks completed the circle. I offered cornmeal to the four directions and fell into a state of prayer and gratefulness: grateful for the gift of soft feathers, grateful to the life of the flicker, grateful for this sacred spot on the earth, grateful for my eyes, my senses, my body being at this place at this time.

I watched the wind blow the central feathers and watched the way light played upon them. I thought about the bird, its death and consumption by an animal, the gift that it left behind. The wind moved the feathers as if they now belonged to a spirit bird. I blessed the bird's life and asked for the continuation of its life. As I looked at the mandala I heard the words, "This is your home," and saw images of golden corn. I sang a song of gratefulness. As I listened to the feathers I heard a high and ethereal sound resonating from them. It was too high to sing. I contented myself with singing a song of the many things I am grateful for. I caught the sun's rays in my hands and felt blessed.

As I played the frog ocharina, the women slowly returned, one by one, to our starting circle in the pine grove. Each woman took us to her sacred spot she had found, introducing it to us and explaining how she would like our participation as she sang her song or read her poem.

The first woman took us to an old alligator juniper tree in the west. "The tree itself is the mandala, it needed nothing more except a blessing of cornmeal," she told us. She showed us the erotic form of the tree's trunk and branches, inviting us to feel both the smooth and the rough places on the tree. She then sat in the branches, cradled by the tree. She told us that as a child she loved climbing trees and finding secret places under grape vines. With the tree supporting her she sang us her song, the first song she had ever written. She sang about the tree as a survivor, she told about the wrinkled cracked skin like that of an elephant, and she sang of the soft underbelly of the skin. As she looked up she sang to the "antlers" of the tree and told us of the strength she felt as the tree cradled her. As her song ended she climbed down from the tree. We placed our hands on the tree, thanking the spirit of the tree. As we thanked the tree a hawk came and circled us and then circled the pine grove where we began our journey.

Our next journey took us south. We hiked down from the pine grove to a sloping area of trees where the next woman had made a red rock heart around three pine trees. She invited us to step inside the heart and find a place to sit. She read a poem which she titled, "The Heart of the Matter." She asked us to dig down into the earth and notice how the pine needles had become part of the earth. She asked us to listen to the wind blowing through the branches of the trees. She asked us to look up and see the sunlight shining on the needles at the top of the trees. Then she asked us to find some natural objects... rocks, sticks, pine cones, bushes... to make sound with as she conducted our forest orchestra. We played our earth music and laughed inside the Heart, inside our hearts.

The next woman took us to the north near another alligator juniper tree. She arranged a very intricate mandala around a tall white wild flower in its brittle fall state. Sticks, rocks, pine needles, and leaves from plants were arranged very carefully. We saw a variety of textures as we looked down upon this autumn mandala. She sang a song about the Ancient One, an animal spirit who had come to her as she sat in this place. She had never written a song before or sung before a group of people. This was a first for her and a risk. We felt honored to receive her song. We thanked the spirit of the Ancient One.

Next we went to my place in the east. As we drew close to the feather mandala I asked everyone to close their eyes. We walked carefully over and formed a circle around the feathers. I asked everyone to first look down and then to open their eyes. There were *ooohhs* and *aaahhs* at the sight of the colorful feathers. We all sat and I gave them each a flicker feather. One woman said flickers are birds of the hearth. I told them how I'd heard the words "This is your home." We sat in silence and watched the feathers blowing gently in the wind. We lightly stroked ourselves with the feathers as I sang my song:

O Mother I am grateful for my life
O Mother I am grateful for this earth
O Mother I am grateful for your warmth
O Mother I am grateful for the sky
O Mother I am grateful. . . .
O Mother I am grateful. . . .

We gave thanks for the flicker.

Then we walked to the oldest tree in the forest, an ancient alligator juniper that I call the Grandmother Tree. We gave her an offering of cornmeal while asking to pick some of the cedar that grows around her. We asked for her blessing and slowly gathered cedar as we sang our way back to my house, filled with the songs and scents of the forest.

Sing For The Earth— Part 2

When we approach the earth with reverence, mysterious things happen to us. When we approach the earth with an attitude of listening, something speaks to us. When we go to Nature to let go of our little self, a greater reality fills us. This earth is ready to draw closer to us when we are ready to draw closer to it. The ways of diversity and interconnectedness are right before us.

In early April 1993, a group of five women rode out together to the Superstition Mountains in Arizona to sing for the earth. During the ride we sang chants to get us out of the daily chit-chat and into the atmosphere of focused intention and unity that chanting can bring. Eyes softened, faces relaxed. As we got closer to the Superstitions, I asked each woman to look at the mountain and to silently say her intention for the day in her heart. Closer still we entered into the desert and found wild flowers beside the road.

As we turned from the main road onto the long and bumpy dirt road that led to the trailhead our faces brightened and the mood became lighter. What do you see when you look at the approaching mountain? Turtle? Guardians? Bear? Fred Flintstone? Ancient man of the rocks, rising out of the bedrock? Where's Dino? To me the mountain looks like a dragon's head, a water serpent, Quetzacoatl.

As we began to hike the trail, we stopped to say our intentions for the day— to rest in the peace of nature; to find our voice; to listen for a song; to connect with the earth of childhood; to let nature speak; to let go of the worries of town; to each find her way. The Superstitions are rich with the legend of the Lost Dutchman's gold mine. "There is gold to be mined today from this mountain, the creative gold that lives inside you. That's what we're seeking."

We walk up the trail past jumping cholla, past saguaro, past cactus flowers, poppies and joshua trees to an outcropping of rocks. Here we make cornmeal bundles and honor the four directions, sing to the wide expanse of air, sing to the copper rocks, sing to the desert. I ask each woman to listen inside for the direction that calls to her. We share what we have heard. One woman cries because she can't find her voice. The keeper of her voice is not ready to be seen or heard. She responds to the south. I tell her about frog . . . the frog in the throat is also the singer who brings cleansing and healing. Perhaps frog will come today.

We continue on the trail until we come to a stream. I teach an old song form the Incredible String Band . . . "water, water, see the water flow, glancing, dancing, see the water flow, oh wizard of changes, teach me the lesson of flowing. . ."[8] Teach us to flow with our own creativity, teach us to flow with our feelings, teach us to flow with our song. I ask each woman to find a spot where she can be alone with nature for an hour. "Let yourself be drawn to a place and in that place offer a cornmeal blessing, listen for what that place has to tell you, listen for a poem or a song. In an hour I'll be playing a frog ocharina to bring us all back to this spot." Each went in her own direction.

I was drawn to a large outcropping of rock, close enough to be by the stream where I could hear it, but also very contained by a circle of rocks, sand and plants. I looked at the large rock, felt its rough surface, sat by its massive presence, gave it an offering of driftwood, fallen flowers, cornmeal and water, listened, and listened. I sat by the rock and wrote a poem. Then I sat further back and noticed a lizard doing push-ups on the rock. He crawled all over the surface of the rock, did his push-ups and then disappeared. After a while I went up to the rock and imitated what I saw lizard do. I turned my head and there was lizard close to my face...golden-throated iridescent turquoise-bellied lizard, eye to eye.

After I had my lizard encounter, it was time to gather everyone. I started to play my frog ocharina. At that moment one woman had just given a cornmeal blessing to frogs she had been listening to. In that moment two frogs appeared on a rock in the stream. Two small beautiful frogs with big voices who sang and appeared to stop and listen to the frog song of the ocharina.

Blessings from the frogs.

I continued to play to gather everyone by the rock so that they could receive frog medicine. Everyone wore delight on their faces when they spotted the frogs.

Each woman took us to her spot, introducing it to us, telling us what she had heard, singing or reading her song or poem and inviting us to see this place in nature with new eyes. First we went to an imagined cave near the stream led by a woman who had felt kinship with the west. She invited us into her cave and read a poem "I In My Cave" about the west and the need for protection. "The cave is a resting place, not a dwelling place," she told us. She then led us to a place in the east where she had found sage. We honor the caves within ourselves and the need for rest and protection, she said, we honor the cleansing brought by the east.

Next we were led to a spot by the stream between two rocks where another woman read us a poem about the discovery of water and the playful porpoises she had found inside the water of herself. I taught my song "white dolphin swimming, swimming, swimming, white dolphin swimming into my heart."[9] We honored the water and the playful porpoise within. The water gave her a new "porpoise" in life, to play instead of working so hard.

Further upstream another woman took us to her spot. She also had looked within the water. She looked into more of a still place, rather than a swift moving place. There she found bugs, spiders, little water skimmers; a pool of wonder. She led us in "Oh Great Spirit" after reading a poem about what Great Spirit had taught her, here by this pool of wonder… "Oh Great Spirit, earth and wind and sea, you are inside and all around me."[10] …We honored the gifts within the water.

We followed another woman upstream to a pool. She told us she had immersed herself in the pool to find her breath. She was a woman with a lost voice on a journey to find one. She believed that breath comes as the first voice. She guided us over rocks to a sandy beach where she had drawn and sculpted a mandala in the sand of a snake, an eagle, a turtle and a bear claw. She hummed as she made it and we stood and hummed around her circle of Self. We honored the snake, eagle, turtle and bear within and honored the emerging of a woman's voice. When she spoke of her mandala her voice was strong and clear.

We sang as we hiked back and stopped to watch the changing light spreading over the canyon. We had discovered so many treasures. We had mined the gold of our creativity. When we reached our point of entry, we looked at the posted topography map to see where we had been. As our fingers traced our footsteps we saw with wonder that we had been in Music Canyon by Music Springs near Music Mountain!

Opening quote: Ruth Murray Underhill, *Singing for Power: The Song Magic of the Papago Indians of Southern Arizona,* University of California Press, Berkeley, 1938, p. 25.

1. Zuni Sunrise Song, *Zuni Indians of New Mexico, Sunrise Vision,* Firedrum Music, Soar Records, 1977.
2. Robert Lawlor, *Voices of the First Day: Awakenings in the Aboriginal Dreamtime*, Inner Traditions, Rochester, Vermont, 1991, p. 38.
3. Susan Elizabeth Hale, *Circle The Earth With Song,* cassette tape and liner notes, 1986.
4. Joachim-Ernst Berendt, *Nada Brahma The World Is Sound: Music and the Landscape of Consciousness*, Destiny Books, Rochester, Vermont, 1987, p. 78.
5. Recorded by Prana on Return of the Mayflower, 1987-88, listed in *Circle of Song: Songs, Chants and Dances for Ritual and Celebration,* compiled by Katie Marks, Lenox, Massachussetts, Full Circle Press, 1993, p. 59.
6. Rose May Dance/Starhawk, listed in *Circle of Song: Songs, Chants and Dances for Ritual and Celebration* compiled by Katie Marks, Lenox, Massachussetts, Full Circle Press, 1993, p. 12.
7. Elizabeth Roberts and Elias Amidon (eds.), *Earth Prayers from Around the World: 365 Prayers, Poems and Invocations for Honoring the Earth,* Harper SanFrancisco, San Francisco, 1991, p. 137.
8. Robin Williamson, The Incredible String Band, *The Hangman's Beautiful Daughter*, Elektra Entertainment, 1968.
9. Susan Elizabeth Hale, *Circle the Earth with Song*, cassette tape, 1986.
10. Anonymous, *Circle of Song: Songs, Chants, and Dances for Ritual and Celebration,* compiled by Katie Marks, Full Circle Press, Lenox, Massachussetts, 1993, p. 118.

Ritual Voices

"And so I greet you
and all the other goddesses
with this song
but it was for you that I began
Now, having begun,
I'll do another for you"
The Hymn to Artemis (Homeric)

Every culture on the face of the earth, from the earliest times to today, has used ritual to give form to its beliefs, enact its myths, grieve its losses, and celebrate its joys. Rituals create stories that act as guiding principles for a person, or a culture. Ritual acts as the concrete embodiment of a story through the use of symbols, art, movement, poetry, music and prayer. Song has always been an integral part of ritual. Song has a unifying function and takes us out of our small selves and brings us in touch with the greater mystery of life. Often the words of the songs tell the story that is being enacted. Songs in rituals are a way to reach out and touch heaven, they help bring heaven down to earth. Singing makes words and prayers live.

Rituals may be very simple. They can be as simple as singing thanks over a meal or as simple as singing a song at sunrise. A ritual can be as simple as blessing a baby by singing its name.

Rituals can be complex and elaborate. These rituals become part of a larger ceremonial cycle. For the Hopi, a cycle of ceremonies is performed throughout the year "in honor of the major forces associated with central elements in the tribe's practical and spiritual life."[1]

The Apache Mountain Spirit Dance takes place over four days and four nights to initiate young maidens into womanhood. Gan dancers offer blessings to the initiate and the tribe. "A chorus and drummer accompany the dancers with songs handed down from generation to generation."[2]

The Navajo Night Chant "opens at sundown and closes eight-and-a-half days later at sunrise."[3] The Night Chant is performed for the benefit of healing a patient who commissions the ceremony on his or her own behalf. At the beginning of the ceremony, a crier stands at the door, calling, "Come on the trail of song."[4]

Sometimes we need to invent our own rituals. These can be opportunities to enact personal stories or address larger issues pressing on our immediate communities. Sometimes they are created by the participants in the emotional moment of the event. Just the coming together for the ritual can be powerful and act as a catalyst.

I have created, performed, or participated in many rituals over the past few years. Often they are more powerful, unique, or magical than I could ever have predicted. Here are several which I found quite special—

The Ritual of the Seven Moons

During the last year-and-a-half I have had many dreams about singing. In these dreams is an image of something which stops me from allowing the full power of my voice. I felt that I needed to shout "I am free!" I knew I needed to enact the dream in my waking life. In one of these dreams was the image "Seven Moons of my People" and the phrase "when the intention is concentrated enough in ritual, each step you take benefits all living things." I connected this with seven feelings, then with the seven chakras of the human body. Instead of writing songs I would let seven songs emerge spontaneously on the night of the event. I envisioned a gathering called *Harvesting the Song*. I sent an invitation to some close women friends and timed the event to take place when the full Taurus moon was in conjunction with my moon. Taurus is the astrological sign that rules the throat and voice. My invitation read:

I am ready now to sing my song for a close group of women friends to witness. I am harvesting my song.
I invite you to share this experience with me.
I will be improvising seven songs out of the moment.
Please bring ten beads. We will be making song necklaces.

The evening of the ritual I lit my office with candles and decorated it with Indian corn. In the center was a Tibetan bowl full of yellow corn beads. As we gathered I passed a corn rattle asking each woman for her support as I took this new step in my life. I spoke of my dream. Then I tied a red silk cord around my neck and covered my face with a veil. I lifted the veil and read a poem I had written with imagery from dreams:

You've strangled me into silence
beheaded me
I've been hung
stabbed in the throat
had my tongue cut out
and still you can't keep me from singing

You've covered my mouth with a veil
put a red hot poker to my throat
and still my song flies on
and is free

No longer can you silence me
No longer can you keep me from
  speaking
  articulating
  singing my song
  loud and strong
  letting the tones trill through my throat
  my power emerging to be heard

To be a singer is to be blessed
honored by life
to move others
to move oneself
by a pure mystery of sound

I function life with my voice
I function life with my words
I function life with my song

I am free of you at last
  black silencer
  black veil
  black blade
  black hand
you've tried in every way you can
to take my voice
and still my song pours forth

I shout my freedom
I sing my song
and I speak for beauty in the world
I heal myself with my voice
I allow the river of life
to flow through my body
to vibrate every cell

I am song
I am strong
I am a singer of life
I am a singer of truth
I am a singer of peace
I am a singer of compassion
I am a singer of heart

My throat is like honey
My song is grain to feed a hungry world
My song is fresh water to quench thirsty souls
And I will sing
with every fiber of my being

Radiance
Radiance
pulsing stream
of my life's blood

When the poem was finished, I took off the cord from around my neck and proclaimed,

"The cord has been cut. I am a singer of life."

I stood up and listened for seven songs, listening to each of my seven chakras and voicing what I heard inside. Each toning was different. Each one was difficult to describe in words. Some emerged with tones and movement. Some had words and tunes. When I listened to my throat chakra something dramatic happened. My left hand rose spontaneously over my head. It was as if I had a rope in my hand and was being hung, killed for my beliefs. My left hand stayed up in the air but turned into a fist. I felt rising anger and began to voice my rage. I let out deep loud sounds and encouraged everyone to join with me.

We toned together and as we toned I sang "no more will we be treated as victims," crying out against rape, murder and abuse women have endured through centuries. As I voiced this in its full power with the support of my friends' voices, the tones began to change. It moved into a song about the gifts we have to share as women, the blessings we bring with our vision, beauty, gentleness and song. Spontaneously everyone joined hands and heard their own beauty and strength validated through my song.

As I listened to the 6th chakra a different song emerged with the words:

I see, I see a world of beauty
I see, I see a world of beauty
Do you see, do you see this world of beauty?
It is here, it is now
Reach out you can touch this world of beauty
It is real, it is here
It is here for all of us to feel

And this world of beauty existed in the room, through my voice, in the faces of the women witnessing. We could each touch this vision and add our own wish to create this world more firmly, more fully in the outside world.

The 7th chakra sound was so high I couldn't duplicate it with my voice. I chimed Tibetan cymbals over each woman's head so she could hear the purity of the ringing sounds which I was hearing.

We ended by making song necklaces. As I passed the corn beads in the Tibetan bowl I invited each woman to strike the bowl to hear it ring, then take a bead and string it on the thread provided. We repeated this process until we had each received a bead from each woman. Each had a story to tell about her bead:

- a corn bead reminds us of this evening and the rich harvest of songs and stories we each have inside

- a wooden bead reminds us of the strength and living energy of the trees
- a multi-colored bead from a large craft shop reminds us of the everyday magic found all around us
- a bead from Afghanistan reminds us of the beauty of other cultures
- a bead blessed by a Tibetan monk reminds us of the beauty of different religions
- beads from New Mexico remind us of our diversity
- little bells remind us of the music of our lives

As we placed the beginnings of our song necklaces around our necks, each woman voiced whatever she wanted to through words, tone or song. I encouraged each woman to continue to add beads to her necklace whenever she took a risk to voice something important in her life. We noticed that this evening there were seven women present, seven beads, seven songs for the dream of the seven moons. Someone commented that it was seven months after my birthday. That night I made a commitment to do this ritual seven times "for the benefit of all living things."

My song necklace is now complete. I have performed *Harvesting the Song* six more times. During the last ritual I burned the red silk cord. It took a long time to burn and became a glowing, red snake that faded into black ashes. Like a snake shedding its skin my voice has been transformed over this two-year process.

Each time different songs have emerged. Each time I felt more free to voice what I heard inside with the full power of my voice. Each time the stories, voices and beads of the women were different. Each evening has been a magical unveiling. Each time I've enacted this ritual I am reminded of the words from the dream: "when the intention is concentrated enough in ritual each step you take benefits all living things."

The Light at the End of the Day

I lived in Lawrence, Kansas when the movie *THE DAY AFTER* was being filmed. This is the story about the day after a nuclear war. Mushroom clouds explode over Kansas landscapes. These were the landscapes I drove past every day. Blackened buildings and burnt cars were on the streets where I shopped every day. Shanty towns of cardboard and tin by the river were looked at every day. As the movie was being filmed the people of Lawrence, Kansas were confronted with these images every single day. Most streets looked normal but sometimes as we turned the corner the scene of a bleak nuclear nightmare would confront us. Could this happen? Could this happen here? The images said "Yes!" There was fear in the air.

During this time I was working with a performance artist named Marsha Paludan. She had gathered a small group of men and women to co-create a performance-ritual around this movie and the issues of war and peace that it raised. We wanted to create a piece that would confront these issues but one that would also instill hope as our town went into viewing *THE DAY AFTER*.

Each time we met we talked about war and peace and then improvised in movement and sound until the performance-ritual had shaped itself out of the mutual interaction of our bodies, hearts and minds. In our discussions we did not ask the big questions of how to stop war but the smaller questions of how do we stop the war within ourselves? How is it that we divide ourselves into an *us-them* mentality in our daily lives? Where is the trigger in each of us that has the capability of wreaking destruction? What brings peace in our lives? How do we live out of a sense of peace that is real? How can we bring peace to the world if we can't bring it to ourselves, our relationships, our families, or our jobs?

We all wanted this peace but we also found the shadow places inside of ourselves: places of gossip, jealousy, fear, greed, racism, hate. We talked about the impact of the small: the one shattered atom that can destroy life, the one voice that radiates peace, the power of each voice to make a difference in the world with its explosion of ideas, compassion and love. We talked about the metaphor of radiation and asked how can we radiate peace into the world. What is it that brings the radiance of spirit in our lives?

We danced and toned and sang these questions until a story emerged with answers told in song and movement.

The story told of a village of people who sowed seed, reaped grain, made bread, washed clothes by the river and sang of the waters flowing. We dressed simply, our only props were wooden dowels and sheer white cloths which became everything we needed to show the simple acts of daily life. Our only accompaniment was the sound of a Tibetan bowl. With the sticks we formed a boat, as we rowed we chanted "we're in this boat together". Joyfully at first, glad to be together, but then, feeling the crowdedness of this all-too-human boat, we began to push and shove and elbow each other. We tumbled out of the boat, grabbed our sticks to defend the right to our territory. The Tibetan bowl clanged loudly as we engaged in battle. We shouted accusations of "Them." As the battle raged, one woman gradually distanced herself from the group long enough to see what was happening. She said "Stop" in a strong but gentle voice and walked into the center of the battle to lay down her weapon. She slowly spiraled inward and sang a Buddhist chant; the heart sutra of Kuan Yin:

Gate gate paragate
Parasamgate
Bodhi Svaha[5]

which translates as:

Gone gone gone beyond
Gone beyond the beyond
to Buddhahood (completely gone)
So be it.[6]

As this chant was intoned each person slowly began to lay down his or her stick, forming a star pattern when all sticks were together. The villagers spiraled inward and joined the chant, adding harmonies and improvising words:

We are they
We are one
We are they
We are one
Gate gate paragate
Parasamgate
Jesu Christe…
Kyrie Eleison…
Ave Maria…
Hare Krishna…
Hallelujah

Together we held the star high singing Hallelujah and placed it in front of what looked like a draped body. Still singing, but allowing the Hallelujah to become more staccato, we turned and walked from the body. A fool greeted us carrying a bundle on her back which she unfolded in front of us. We circled around this bundle and unfolded a large parachute. The parachute was filled with colored feathers which we tossed into the air. Our Hallelujah chant gave way to A-ha-ha-ha-ha-ha-ha-ha Ah ha-ha-ha-ha-ha-ha-ha. . . . Gradually the parachute and feathers fell to the floor. The Tibetan bowl rang and an old woman arrived with a basket of apples, followed by children ringing bells. They circled us and then gradually took audience members by the hand to join us in our ever-widening circle. We ended by singing:

> We have gathered
> Singing together together
> We are one voice
> Singing forever forever[7]

The body near the star was undraped to reveal baskets of homemade bread which we shared with the audience in a feast of bread and apples.

"The Light at the End of the Day" was performed the night before *THE DAY AFTER* was aired on television. As we watched the mushroom clouds billow over our town they were superimposed with the image of a billowing parachute dancing in joy. The horror of a dying world was superimposed with the images of children ringing bells and affirming life.

Several days later a small group of dancers and townspeople met by the river at the site of the shanty town for a ritual to continue to heal the images of *THE DAY AFTER*. The ritual started with the ringing of the Tibetan bowl. As the bowl was being played, it began to rain gently. The raindrops radiated circles in the river water. All of our intentions are contained within this circle. We allow the healing to spread out from us. One of the dancers began to speak and cry. Her tears mingled with the rain. As we spread grass seed onto the ground that had housed the shanty town it was as if the scattered seeds looked like tears and rain. We spread the seeds onto the earth in ever-widening circles, sowing our prayers of peace as we sang.

Valentine for Bosnia

In January '93 I received a flyer from a friend:

> *"In response to continued reports from Bosnia concerning the systematic rape and torture of women and children in the name of 'ethnic cleansing', several women's groups in Santa Fe, New Mexico are joining together to send our sisters in former Yugoslavia a Valentine present. At 3:00 pm Mountain Standard Time on February 13, 1993, upwards of 250 women will gather in Santa Fe for a healing ritual. At which time we will be sending our love and prayers to Bosnia. It is our intention to transform the rage and pain we feel, in response to this shocking situation, to compassion and action to see that it stops."*

At the designated time, 25 women gathered in the Manzano mountains outside of Albuquerque to send our Valentine to

Bosnia. We sat in the form of a heart and toned, sending the compassion through our voices to the women and children in Bosnia, to all women and children of the world, to the husbands, brothers and fathers and to the men who rape.

Sounds came from the heart, sounds first of grief and pain, sounds of strength and power, sounds that became softer at the end as we sent love through our voices. After we toned I asked each woman to lift up her hands to feel our sounds still vibrating in the center of our hearts and send it to all those who need compassion and healing.

As each woman spoke, she sent our singing valentine to many places— to Bosnia and Northern Ireland, to South Africa and city streets, to institutions and nursing homes, to abused children and those that abuse them.

We spoke names of friends, husbands, mothers, grandmothers, children . . . and to all those unnamed who live within our hearts. We brought our hands down and placed them on the ground to send our song to the earth. Together we sang:

> Listen listen listen . . .
> Listen listen listen . . .
> Listen listen listen
> to my heart song
> Listen listen listen
> to my heart song
> I will never forget you
> I will never forsake you
> I will never forget you
> I will never forsake you[8]

As we sang we spontaneously clasped hands forming a living heart of song. Many eyes were wet with tears, many women still crying, touched both by our own interconnectedness with each other and the women of Bosnia. "I will never forget you, never forsake you, never forget you, never forsake you. . . ." The song faded and slowly we began to talk of what had happened:

One woman saw a Bosnian girl and imagined holding her as she cried. Another sent love to the men who rape. She said she could finally live with the darkness of her own rape and now had compassion for men who live from a place of darkness.

As we continued to share the rest of the day the image of stone soup came to mind. Stone soup is the children's story of a hungry peasant. He conjures up the image of a wonderful soup as he talks to the town. He offers a stone to the soup pot. Everyone else is to bring something different to put in the soup. At the end, a delicious soup is made which is shared by everyone in town. Often women feel they're not offering much or apologize about what they are offering. Often this "stone" is the catalyst for a rich sharing. Many had talked earlier of the emotional soup in which they felt they were swimming. Someone passed a stone in the shape of a heart and as we added our words, tears and songs we realized we had created a feast from the sharing of stone soup.

Singing Corridors

On Earth Day of 1993, fifty singers, led by myself and Forrest Evans, gathered in a resonant corridor in an Art Deco shopping center. We gathered to sing for the earth, allowing our love for the earth to ring through our voices, sending it out through the corridors to radiate out into Albuquerque and beyond. We sent out the vibrations of our healing intentions through our voices. The corridor echoed, rang, soared with our song, a pure tunnel of sweet song rich with overtones. Layer upon layer of sound mingled high above us in the corridor, moving some to tears and others to rapture. The toning became softer until it became a hush.

Out of the hush came Forrest's beautiful tenor voice:

"Oh Mother don't you weep, for there are those who care,
Oh Mother don't you weep, for there are those who care.
I can hear your cries like my own.
I can hear your cries."[9]

And 50 of "those who cared" joined in the song. As we sang others came near to listen. Some came in to join the singing.

"The earth is a woman and she will rise.
The earth is a woman and she will rise.
We will live in her.
We will live in her."[10]

As we sang I could feel the body of our song giving body to Mother Earth, giving her the nourishment of our soul song.

In our singing we took the courage of our collective voices to say that we *do* believe in the healing power of song, we *do* believe in sending our intentions out of the world through our voices. Our singing was an act of magic; the old deep magic that lives within our bones and stirs us alive as we sing together.

With the power of this magic we call for the return of the elements:

"The earth, the water, the fire, the air,
Return, return, return, return."[11]

Return the cleansing waters. Return the pure sweet air. Return the fires of creativity, return the sacred earth. Return to a way of living with the seasons. Return to a deeper listening, a deeper compassion for all living things, all plants, animals, birds, insects, all living things. Return to a deeper way of knowing. We sang and improvised harmonies, rhythms, new words, new ways of singing, new ways of listening. And as we continued to sing many chants, spontaneous dancing broke out at the ends and in the center of the corridor. A clown came and danced, inviting others to follow. Singing faces, dancing feet, delight, and joy shone on the faces of those watching, listening, and singing.

"I can feel your heart beat,
I can feel your heartbeat,
I can feel your heartbeat,
heartbeat, heartbeat, Mother Earth."

We ended with a Seneca song to the Moon, a gentle lullaby. The words "Neesa Neesa Neesa Gai we o" mean "Winter Moon. The Creator is in everything."[12] We slowly formed a circle within the corridor and Forrest and I went up each side with a lit candle. We lit the candles of the singers, and gazed into the light from many eyes as we passed by singing. When we finished I asked the singers to leave at their own time, taking their light and their song with them out into the world. Toning started again on its own. Some left soon. Others remained for another 20 minutes to sing and linger in the healing balm of song.

Ritual Voices

Opening Quote: Charles Boer (trans.), *The Homeric Hymns*, Swallow Press, Chicago, 1970, p. 7.

1. Jamake Highwater, *Rituals of the Wind: North American Indian Ceremonies, Music and Dance*, Alfred Van Der Marck Editions, New York, 1984, p. 83.
2. Ibid., p. 65.
3. Ibid., p. 39.
4. Ibid.
5. *Sufi Dance and Song*, Volume Two, Sufi Islamia/Prophecy Publications, San Francisco, California, 1982, p. 46.
6. Ibid.
7. A song learned in a "Dances for Universal Peace" gathering in northern California in 1970.
8. Parmahansa Yogananda, from Anna Kealoha's *Songs of the Earth: Music for the World*, Celestial Arts, Berkeley, 1989, p. 139.
9. Anonymous, learned in Albuquerque, New Mexico.
10. Dakota Butterfield, from *Libana, Fire Within*, Ladyslipper, Durham, North Carolina, 1990, p. 139.
11. Anonymous, *Circle of Song: Songs, Chants and Dances for Ritual and Celebration*, compiled by Kate Marks, Full Circle Press, Lenox, Massachussetts, 1993, p. 57.
12. Ibid., p. 143.

My Song Journey (2)

"The magnetic songlines guided the physical ceremonial journeys of the tribes. Initiated men and women learned to travel these subtle and invisible energy veins using their psychic or spirit body. Thus they were able to exchange songs, dances, and mythic visions of the ever unfolding Dreamtime reality over great distances. Tribal elders claim that not only Australia but the entire earth, at one time, was linked through the songlines."

Robert Lawlor

The idea of hidden songlines alive and singing in the earth is a powerful image. I am reminded of Kokopelli's trail, planting songseeds in the earth to create songlines. I wonder if the ancient roads leading to the Anasazi ruins of Chaco Canyon are songlines? How many places are songlines that we rush over and don't take the time to listen to? What are the songlines we are creating in our lives? Are we adding to the resonance of the earth as we travel or are we just creating more static? We have credit lines, bottom lines, deadlines. Where are the songlines?

This chapter continues my own song journey. I believe a song journey exists for each of us. As we discover our own song journey we find ourselves back in the world with a restored voice, feet solid on the ground— magic happening around us, all the time. I believe we can create songlines, perhaps not in the same way as the Aborigines, but with our own intent and vision.

Think of any trip you take as a songline that can add to the vibration around that place to function the life there. When I'm invited to teach in another city or state I concentrate my intention and voice to create songlines between my home and my destination. I have created songlines between my home in Sandia Park and Albuquerque; between Sandia Park and Scottsdale, Arizona; and between my home and Vancouver, British Columbia. Singing is part of the journey, whether in a car or walking on a trail; singing what I feel in response to nature; stopping at natural landforms, mountains, canyons, rivers, waterfalls, springs and singing to the spirit of the place; offering blessings to the nature spirits; all these help to create songlines on the earth and in your life. It helps me to trust in the magic of singing. Songlines create a magnetic resonance that puts you in the right place at the right time, to say the right thing and to call forth the right action. Magic does happen. Song brings magic. I would like to tell you a story from my life, a story about trusting in the magic of song.

During the summer of 1993, I had been asked to teach a week-long *Finding Your Voice* class in Colorado as I had the year before. A close friend had also been asked to teach. I asked her if she would like to drive up a few days early. I had been told that I would need to take my chances in offering a workshop in the small town of Paonia, Colorado. I could have 20 people show up or no one at all. Trust in the magic. We decided to go and take our chances. My friend loves to sing. While driving to Paonia we sang every song that came to mind: show tunes, chants, Joni Mitchell songs, lullabies. We hummed and made up songs in the car. Our singing helped her to heal bad memories of taking car trips with her family when she was growing up. She confided that she dreaded car trips because her family often bickered. She said that this was the easiest trip she had ever taken because of all the singing.

On the day of the workshop only two people came. I was disappointed but decided to enjoy the extra time as a vacation. We decided to nose around the two block town. We went into a few shops, browsed. My friend, somewhat bored, asked if I was ready to leave. "No, let's complete the circle, let's go to that building over there." Complete the circle. Most rituals have some sort of circumambulation, walking a circle in prayer, dancing a circle, singing a circle, creating a songline. Magic spoke to me unawares. I thought it was just a figure of speech at the time, but now I know I was pulled in by the magnetic resonance of my songline. Somehow I needed to complete a circle and the building I pointed to was part of that completion.

We passed through the door into an art gallery. We were greeted by a man. He seemed very familiar. I knew there were old places between us, messages needed to be retrieved and spoken. Something of the past and the future spoke within my intuition. When I walked into the gallery and saw him all this registered in an instant. He asked me if I like photography and took a black portfolio out from beneath the counter. He opened the book into image after image of cobalt blue light, water, and rocks. Places I have seen inside my own bones... Cave crone, water deva, blue rock spirit images evoked out of landscape and camera... I felt I could sing them. These were not flat photographs, but three dimensional mythic stories. "I know how to sing these," I said. He looked at me quizzically. (Later, he would ask me if I offered this to everyone I met.) He turned off the radio and dimmed the lights. I looked at one of the photographs and brought its imprint inside, imagining the breath of water and rock. I felt this as a pool of sound and began to sing in a way I had never experienced before. Nature spirits vibrated within me and I sang higher than I normally go. My companion described it as soul-searing, a hymn triumphantly emerging out of the ground. When I opened my eyes all three of us stood covered with goosebumps. The photographer looked at me and said, "I've been waiting for you."

He wanted these pictures to have more than a gallery showing. Something else needed to be involved with them. When he heard me sing he realized that they needed to be shown in a different context. He imagined showing them as slides on silk swaying in the dark with me singing behind them, giving voice to the living presence of the canyon where the photographs came from.

I said YES!

On the way back to New Mexico, my friend and I stopped at the place where the photographs had been taken and I sang there. After seeing the flat surfaces of the photographs it felt wonderful to be in the true environment. I sang in response to its spirit. There was one very large boulder that drew me to sing its low pulse. I knew the next step was to meet the photographer here and sing together. I asked for a blessing for this newly born collaboration.

This entire sequence of events happened through taking risks to move my own song journey one step further into the unknown. I had never done anything like this before. I had never approached a stranger with the seemingly odd request of— "Excuse me, I'd like to sing your photographs." There was no context in my society to support what I did. I had never heard of anyone doing anything like this. But something in me trusted in my own song journey enough to open up and let the creative energy flow. I was ready to take this step and sing in a new way. It was as if the ancient voices were speaking to me asking me to allow them to sing through me. I trusted in the magic of the moment.

An entire new song path has begun to unfold, a collaboration with many exciting possibilities. This anecdote shows how we may never know *exactly* where things are heading, but opportunities emerge every time. Trusting in the greater process manifests our destiny. I believe as we track the songline we will find the places of the greatest resonance and know where to go next. My voice has been restored to new dimensions. My faith in the magic of singing has deepened.

Opening quote: Robert Lawlor, *Voices of the First Day: Awakenings in Aboriginal Dreamtime*, Inner Traditions, Rochester, Vermont, 1991, p. 126.

Restored Voices

"It's just a breath and it's my breath
It's just a word and it's my word
It's just a song and it's my song
It's just a voice and it's my voice
My voice, my voice
Rejoice, Rejoice!"
Victoria Wolcott

Over and over again, I hear from students that what restores their voices is not some secret technique but an atmosphere of safety and permission to explore their inner sounds. Our first sounds are often tentative and quavering. My main task is to establish a safe space for someone to sing. The more that safe place is provided where students can take risks and expose their voices, the more the safe space becomes internalized. People can then carry that feeling with them wherever they go. Initial fears may still accompany the act of singing before new people. But we can also remember the times when we were heard, listened to and accepted. The fear then becomes fuel for the song. What has helped me in the restoration of my voice is to know that I am not alone when I sing, that a Greater Spirit is there in the breath which supports my song. The same Spirit is part of all of us, all of our voices, and all of our songs.

What is a restored voice? This is a voice that knows it has the choice to speak and to sing as well as to be silent. It is a voice with momentum that moves from the inside to the outside world without stopping through the layers of critics and silencers. It is a voice that can respond back and hold onto its truth in the midst of inner or outer criticism. Maybe it is a voice that loves the feeling of singing and doesn't judge how it sounds. Perhaps it is a voice that wants to be heard and takes the risk to be heard in spite of any fear. It is a voice that knows it has something to give and so it reaches out. It is a person who lives his or her sound in the world. Living one's sound in the world can take many forms. For some it has given them courage to join a choir, to sing a solo in a play, to leave a song message over the phone, to offer to sing at a funeral, to sing alone in nature, to include chanting in morning meditations, or to tone everyday as a practice. One woman told me "I have toning with me 24 hours a day. It's always there to help me."

When people rediscover their voices, they often find them changed. The highs and lows have been restored, their voices are fuller with more harmonics. Different nuances are felt and acknowledged. "My voice can do a lot more than just sing! It's bigger and stronger, there's more of me in it." Even people who have been in choirs for years will express dramatic changes. "My voice is truly mine. It's powerful, beautiful, a delight-maker, a source of joy for me," another woman said.

For some, toning has been the foundation for their own personal healing. People have told me that they had felt frozen, numb, asleep, or didn't know how to express themselves emotionally. A woman remarked that when she first began to tone she experienced a painful unthawing, but as her fears melted she was revived and a flatness of tone grew to a full range of emotion. "I didn't know who I was. I hadn't heard my true self. How can I stand up for myself if I don't know who I really am? Now I have my voice back!"

Sometimes finding our true voice allows us to move on, in spite of our fears, to the next step in life. A sense of trust blossoms about decisions we have to make. Toning can go to areas of old pain, shake them up, move them around. "Through toning I've been able to acknowledge that my grief is real, my areas of stuckness are real and I can still go forward." Perhaps we reach a level of hidden secrets and they are revealed as unproductive. "I've reached a new sense of honesty with myself and the people I love. My sorrows are not gone but the shame and guilt have been erased."

To free the person by freeing the voice carries over into relationships with others. To own our voice gives us a center in dealing with the realities of the world. One woman has found that she uses song directly in her marriage— she vocalizes her emotion in arguments "when I can't find words to express my anger, or if the only words that come out are abusive. My marriage has become much more vocal, now we even groan together!" I have often wondered what the world would be like if we took a cue from opera and sang to each other in the pitched battles of our disagreements.

Learning to express one's emotional truth through sound has allowed some women to confront difficult situations. Momentum can be gathered before confrontations occur. A woman from my singing group found the courage at a Peacemaker's Circle to confront three teenage boys who robbed her and her son at gunpoint. The Peacemaker's Circle is a Navajo form of tribal justice. Tribal elders, the boys and their families met with this woman and her son, her family and friends at her request. Everybody was heard. The woman and her son voiced their pain and anger over the robbery and asked for alternative punishment and compensation for the damage done. The mothers voiced their anguish about their sons' behavior. The sons apologized and agreed to the punishment. Through this voicing process, the sons were given a opportunity to accept the consequences of their actions and hopefully change their lives. "Even when my voice falters and breaks I know I can find it again. I can forgive myself when it breaks, because I know how to find its beauty."

To once again find our voice restores us in ways we often can't imagine. We trust our intuition, we find connection to real spiritual sources. We enjoy the surprise of discovering the power of our own voices. This leads to more songs more often which leads to more discoveries. Our voices don't have to be perfect, we don't have to be perfect. Our lives are works in progress where risks are taken as we grow in confidence. Singing shows us how we think about ourselves, about the world around us. Each time we sing is a ceremony of our intent and our perceptions.

Now is the time to take singing out of the shower, out of the car, even out of the choir loft and bring it back into our daily lives— where song belongs.

Imagine melodies floating carefree in the hallways at work, snatches of a personal tune on sidewalks, lullabyes at checkout lines in the grocery store, voices of children singing openly without reprimand— in all their diversity, colors of emotion, nuances of praise, the rivers of our inner life flowing once again... *Everyday.*

Each time a person with a restored voice sings, he or she gives permission and safety for others to sing. Each time someone speaks from the heart, we are reminded that we do have that choice. Each time someone touches the source where singing originates— health is brought to the world. Our actions are like dropping a pebble into a pond. Each person who sings from the soul adds to the pond's ripples. Each voice adds to the greater health of our common worlds— and this does make a difference.

A grade school teacher remarked that kids notice how everything she says seems to come out in song and they feel more free about their own voices. We are blessed at birth with the ability to sing. This is our human way to be in the world. All over the world.

All over the world people are singing again.

A woman suddenly realizes "I may not be a great singer, but I am a song." All over the world life is but a song. Cultures who still use song, who know the power of song, know this as fact. Song mixes the inside world into the outer world. Our soul becomes the world's soul, *anima mundi.* How can we keep from singing?

One night a group of men and women walk out
into the desert, form a circle and tone the stars.
Then sit and listen.

The journey ends in silence.

And begins once again.

Opening quote: Victoria Wolcott, a student from my *Finding Your Voice Workshop* at La Foret in Carbondale, Colorado, 1992.

Breathe in

Breathe out

Listen

"I feel a song coming on."

Refrain

Bibliography

VOICE, SONG, AND TONE

Beaulieu, John; *Music and Sound in the Healing Arts;* Station Hill Press, Barrytown, New York, 1987.

Campbell, Don; *The Roar of Silence: Healing Powers of Breath, Tone and Music;* Quest Books, Wheaton, Illinois, 1989.

Chun-Tao Cheng, Stephen; *The Tao of Voice: A New East-West Approach to Transforming the Singing and Speaking Voice;* Destiny Books, Rochester, Vermont, 1991.

David, Nada Foster; *Sing With Your Soul;* Foster David, Roswell, New Mexico, 1979.

Dewhurst-Maddock, Olivea; *The Book of Sound Therapy: Heal Yourself with Music and Voice;* Simon & Schuster, New York, 1993.

Gardner-Gordon, Joy; *The Healing Voice: Traditional and Contemporary Toning, Chanting and Singing;* The Crossing Press, Freedom, California, 1993.

Garfield, Leah Maggie; *Sound Medicine: Healing with Music, Voice and Song;* Celestial Arts, Berkeley, California, 1987.

Goldman, Jonathan; *Healing Sounds: The Power of Harmonics;* Element Books, Shaftesbury, Massachussetts, 1992.

Jindrak, Karel F. and Heda; *Sing, Clean Your Brain and Stay Sound and Sane: Postulate of Mechanical Effect of Vocalization on the Brain;* Jindrak, Forest Hills, New York, 1986.

Jones, Leroi; *Blues People;* Morrow & Co., New York, 1963.

Keyes, Laurel Elizabeth; *Toning: The Curative Power of the Voice;* De Vorss, Santa Monica, 1973.

Linklater, Kristen; *Freeing the Natural Voice;* Drama Book Pub., New York, 1976.

McCallion, Michael; *The Voice Book;* Theatre Arts Books, Routledge, New York, 1988.

Moses, P.J.; *The Voice of Neurosis;* Grune & Stratton, New York, 1954.

Newham, Paul; *The Singing Cure: An Introduction to Voice Movement Therapy;* Shambhala, Boston, 1994.

Ortiz, Simon; *Song, Poetry and Language: Expression and Perception;* Navajo Community College Press, Tsaile, Arizona, 1977.
Pickard, Wayland; *Complete Singer's Guide to Becoming a Working Professional;* Pickard Publishing, Studio City, California, 1992.
Reagon, Bernice Johnson and Sweet Honey in the Rock; *We Who Believe in Freedom: Sweet Honey in the Rock... Still on the Journey;* Doubleday, New York, 1993.
Sokolov, Lisa; *Vocal Revelations: The Therapeutic Process in Finding One's Voice;* Unpublished Master's Thesis, New York University, 1981.
Underhill, Ruth Murray; *Singing For Power: The Song Magic of the Papago Indians of Southern Arizona;* University of California Press, Berkeley, California, 1938.

SONGBOOKS

Bierhorst, John; *A Cry From The Earth: Music of the North American Indians;* Ancient City Press, Santa Fe, New Mexico, 1979.
Blood-Patterson, Peter (editor); *Rise Up Singing;* Sing Out, Bethlehem, Pennsylvania, 1988.
Carawan, Guy and Candie (editors); *We Shall Overcome: Songs of the Southern Freedom Movement;* Oak Publications, New York, 1963.
Curtis, Natalie (editor); *The Indian's Book: Authentic Native American Legends, Lore and Music;* Bonanza Books, New York, 1987.
Kealoha, Anna; *Songs of the Earth: Music of the World;* Celestial Arts, Berkeley, California,1989.
Libana (editors); *Fire Within: Magical and Contemplative Rounds and Songs From Around the World;* Ladyslipper, Durham, North Carolina, 1990.
Lomax, John A. and Alan (editors); *Cowboy Songs and Other Frontier Ballads,* Macmillan, New York, 1986.
Marks, Kate (editor); *Circle of Song: Songs, Chants, and Dances for Ritual and Celebration;* Lenox, Massachussetts, 1993.
Masters, Brian (editor); *The Waldorf Songbook;* Floris Books, Edinburgh, Scotland, 1987.
Maynord, Robert; *Chants For the Journey;* Sacred Arts, Berkeley, California, 1986.

Bibliography

Sorrells, Rosalie (editor); *What, Woman, and Who, Myself, I AM: An Anthology of Songs and Poetry of Women's Experience;* Wooden Shoe, Sonoma, California, 1974.

DANCES OF UNIVERSAL PEACE

Dances of Universal Peace III; Instruction Book; Sufi Islamia/Prophecy Publications; San Francisco, 1985.

Spiritual Dance and Walk: An Introduction from the Work of Murshid Samuel L. Lewis; Sufi Islamia Ruhaniat Society, San Francisco, 1978.

Sufi Dance and Song, Volume 2, Instruction Book; Sufi Islamia Ruhaniat Society, San Francisco, 1982.

MUSIC HEALING AND THERAPY

Andrews, Ted; *Sacred Sounds: Transformation through Music and Word;* Llewellyn Publications, Saint Paul, Minnesota, 1993.

Beaulieu, John; *Music and Sound in the Healing Arts;* Station Hill Press; Barrytown, New York, 1987.

Berendt, Joachim-Ernst; *Nada Brahma The World is Sound: Music and the Landscape of Consciousness;* Destiny Books, Rochester, Vermont, 1987.

Berendt, Joachim-Ernst; *The Third Ear: On Listening to the World;* Element Books, Shaftesbury, Dorset, England, 1988.

Bonny, Helen and Savary, Louis; *Music and Your Mind: Listening with a New Consciousness;* Harper & Row, New York, 1973.

Campbell, Don; *Introduction to the Musical Brain;* Magnamusic-Baton, Inc., St. Louis, 1983.

——— ; *Music: Physician for Times to Come;* Quest Books, Wheaton, Illinois, 1991.

Campbell, Don (editor); *Music and Miracles;* Quest Books, Wheaton, Illinois, 1992.

David, William; *The Harmonics of Sound, Color and Vibration: A System for Self-Awareness and Soul Evolution;* DeVorss and Co., Marina del Rey, California, 1980.

Gardner, Kay; *Sounding the Inner Landscape: Music as Medicine;* Caduceus Publications, Stonington, Maine, 1990.

Gaston, E. Thayor (editor); *Music in Therapy;* Macmillan Co., New York, 1968.

Godwin, Joscelyn; *Harmonies of Heaven and Earth: The Spiritual Dimensions of Music;* Inner Traditions, Rochester, Vermont, 1987.

——— ; *Music, Mysticism and Magic: A Sourcebook*; Arkanaa, New York and London, 1987.

Halpern, Steven with Savary, Louis; *Sound Health: The Music and Sounds that Make Us Whole;* Harper & Row, San Francisco, 1985.

Hamel, Peter Michael; *Through Music to the Self;* Shambhala Publications, Boulder, Colorado, 1979.

Harris, Pamela; *Music and Self: Living Your Inner Sound;* Intermountain Publishing, Albuquerque, New Mexico, 1989.

Hart, Mickey with Stevens, Jay; *Drumming at the Edge of Magic: A Journey into the Spirit of Percussion;* HarperSanFrancisco, San Francisco, 1990.

Katcsh, Shelley and Merle-Fishman, Carol; *The Music Within You;* Simon & Schuster, Inc.; New York, 1985.

Kenny, Carolyn Bereznak; *The Field of Play: A Guide for the Theory and Practice of Music Therapy;* Ridgeview Publishing, Atascadero, California, 1989.

——— ; *The Mythic Artery: The Magic of Music Therapy;* Ridgeview Publishing, Atascadero, California, 1982.

Khan, Sufi Inayat; *Music;* Sufi Publishing Co., New Delhi, India, 1962.

Lingerman, Hal; *The Healing Energies of Music;* Quest Books, Wheaton, Illinois, 1983.

McClellan, Randall; *The Healing Forces of Music: History, Theory and Practice;* Amity House, Amity, New York, 1988.

Menuhim, Yehudi and David, Curtis; *The Music of Man;* Simon & Schuster, New York, 1979.

Merritt, Stephanie; *Mind, Music and Imagery;* Penguin Books, New York, 1990.

——— ; *Successful, Non-Stressful Learning: Applying the Lozanov Method to All Subject Areas*; Learning to Learn, San Diego, 1983.

Moog, H.; *The Musical Experience of the Pre-School;* Schott, London, England, 1975.

Bibliography

Rael, Joseph with Marlow, Mary Elizabeth; *Being and Vibration;* Council Oaks Books, Tulsa, Oklahoma, 1993.

Rudhyar, Dane; *The Magic of Tone and the Art of Music;* Shambhala Publications, Boulder, Colorado, 1982.

Ruud, Even; *Music Therapy and its Relationship to Current Treatment Theories;* Magnamusic-Baton, St. Louis, 1978.

Scott, Cyril; *Music: It's Secret Influence Throughout the Ages;* The Aquarian Press, Wellingborough, Northamptonshire, England, 1958.

Stewart, R.J.; *Music and the Elemental Psyche;* Destiny Books, Rochester, Vermont, 1987.

——— ; *Music, Power, and Harmony: A Workbook of Music and Inner Forces*; Blandford, London, England, 1990.

Thurman, Dr. Leon and Langness, Anne Peter; *Heartsong: A Guide to Active Pre-Birth and Infant Parenting through Language and Singing*; Music Study Services, Englewood, Colorado, 1986.

CHILDREN'S BOOKS

Anderson, Hans Christian; "The Little Mermaid" in *Fairy Tales of Hans Christian Anderson*; Orion Press, New York, 1958.

——— ; *The Nightengale;* Crown Publishers, New York, 1985.

Anderson, Lonzo; *Arion and the Dolphins;* Charles Scribners, New York, 1978.

Burnett, Frances Hodgson; *The Secret Garden;* Harper Trophy, New York, 1991.

Cameron, Anne; *How the Loon Lost Her Voice;* Harbour Publishing Co., Vancouver, British Columbia, 1985.

Cohlene, Terri; *Dancing Drum: A Cherokee Legend;* Watermill Press, Mahwah, New Jersey, 1990.

Courlander, Harold; *The Hat Shaking Dance and Other Ashanti Tales from Ghana;* Harcourt, Brace and World, Inc., New York, 1957.

Duff, Maggie; *Dancing Turtle;* Macmillan Publishing Co., New York, 1981.

Grahame, Kenneth; *The Wind in the Willows;* Charles Scribners, New York, 1960.

Hayes, Joe; *Coyote &: Native American Folktales;* Mariposa Publishing, Santa Fe, New Mexico, 1983.
L'Engle, Madeleine; *A Wrinkle in Time;* Yearling Books, New York, 1962.
——— ; *A Wind in the Door;* Yearling Books, New York, 1973.
——— ; *A Swiftly Tilting Planet;* Farrar, Straus, Giroux, New York, 1978.
——— ; *Dance in the Desert;* Farrar, Straus, Giroux, New York, 1969.
Lopez, Barry; *Crow and Weasel*; North Point Press, Berkeley, 1990.
McNeal, M.E.A.; *The Magic Storysinger: From the Finnish Epic Tale;* Stemmer House, Kalevala, Maryland, 1993.
Milne, A.A.; *The House at Pooh Corner;* Yearling Books, New York, 1970.
Moon, Sheila; *Knee Deep in Thunder;* Guild for Psychological Studies Publishing House, San Francisco, 1986.
——— ; *Hunter Down the Prize;* Guild for Psychological Studies Publishing House, San Francisco, 1986.
Newham, Paul; *The Outlandish Adventures of Orpheus in the Underworld;* Barefoot Books, Boston, 1994.
Robinson, Adjai; *The Stepchild and the Fruit Trees;* Charles Scribners, New York, 1974.
Sheehan, Patty; *Kylie's Song;* Advocacy Press, Santa Barbara, 1988.
——— ; *Kylie's Concert;* Marshmedia, Kansas City, Missouri, 1993.

WOMEN

Allen, Paula Gunn; *Grandmothers of the Light: A Medicine Woman's Sourcebook;* Beacon Press, Boston, 1991.
Claremont de Castillejo, Irene; *Knowing Woman: A Feminine Psychology;* Harper Colophon, New York, 1973.
Duerk, Judith; *Circle of Stones: Woman's Journey to Herself;* Lura Media, San Diego, 1989.
Estes, Clarissa Pinkola; *Women Who Run With the Wolves: Myths and Stories of the Wild Woman Archetype;* Ballantine Books, New York, 1992.
Gilligan, Carol; *In a Different Voice: Psychological Theory and Women's Development;* Harvard University Press, Cambridge, Massachussetts, 1982.
Graves, Robert; *The White Goddess;* Farrar, Strauss, Giroux, New York, 1948.

BIBLIOGRAPHY

Hall, Nor; *The Moon and the Virgin: Reflections on the Archetypal Feminine;* Harper and Row, New York, 1980.

Harding, M. Esther; *Women's Mysteries: Ancient and Modern;* Harper and Row, New York, 1971.

Johnson, Buffie; *Lady of the Beasts: Ancient Images of the Goddess and Her Sacred Animals;* Harper and Row, San Francisco, 1988.

Leonard, Linda Schierse; *The Wounded Woman: Healing the Father-Daughter Relationship;* Shambhala Books, Boulder, 1983.

Markale, Jean; *Women of the Celts*; Inner Traditions, Rochester, Vermont, 1986.

Murdock, Maureen; *The Heroine's Journey: Woman's Quest for Wholeness;* Shambhala Books, Boston, 1990.

Neuman, Erich; *The Great Mother: An Analysis of an Archetype;* Princeton University Press/Bollingen, Princeton, New Jersey, 1963.

Perera, Sylvia Brinton; *Descent to the Goddess: A Way of Initiation for Women;* Inner City Books, Toronto, 1981.

Rush, Anne Kent; *Moon, Moon;* Random House, New York, 1976.

Russell, Sandi; *Render Me My Song: African-American Women Writers from Past to Present;* St. Martin's Press, New York, 1990.

Stone, Merlin; *Ancient Mirrors of Womanhood: Volumes I & II;* Sibylline Books, Village Station, New York, 1979.

Wilson, Annie; *The Wise Virgin: The Missing Link Between Men and Women;* Turnstone Books, 1979.

Woodman, Marion; *Addiction to Perfection: The Still Unravished Bride;* Inner City Books, Toronto, 1982.

———; *The Pregnant Virgin: A Process of Psychological Transformation;* Inner City Books, Toronto, 1985.

RITUAL

Bahti, Tom; *Southwest Indian Ceremonials*; KC Publications, Las Vegas, Nevada, 1982.

Beane, Wendell C. and Doty, William G. (editors); *Myths, Rites and Symbols: A Mircea Eliade Reader: Volumes I & II*; Harper and Row, New York, 1975.

Beck, Renee and Metrich, Sydney Barbara; *The Art of Ritual: A Guide to Creating and Performing Your Own Ceremonies for Growth and Change*; Celestial Arts, Berkeley, California, 1990.

Cahill, Sedonia and Halpern, Joshua; *Ceremonial Circle*; Harper SanFrancisco, San Francisco, 1992.

Easwaran, Eknath; *God Makes the Rivers to Flow*; Blue Mountain Center of Meditation, Berkeley, California, 1982.

Eaton, Evelyn; *I Send a Voice*; Quest Books, Wheaton, Illinois, 1978.

———; *The Shaman and the Medicine Wheel*; Quest Books, Wheaton, Illinois, 1982.

Eliade, Mircea; *Rites and Symbols of Initiation: The Mysteries of Birth and Rebirth*; Harper and Row, New York, 1958.

Frazer, Sir James George; *The Golden Bough: A Study in Magic and Religion*; Macmillan Co., New York, 1951.

Halprin, Lawrence and Burns, Jim; *Taking Part: A Workshop Approach to Collective Creativity*; MIT Press, Cambridge, Massachusetts, 1974.

Harrison, Jane; *Ancient Art and Ritual*; The University Press, Cambridge, Massachusetts, 1913.

Highwater, Jamake; *Ritual of the Wind: North American Indian Ceremonies*; Viking Press, New York, 1977.

———; *Dance: Rituals of Experience*; A & W Publishers, Inc., New York, 1978.

La Chapelle, Dolores and Bourque, Janet; *Earth Festivals: Seasonal Celebrations for Everyone*; Finn Hill Arts, Silverton, Colorado, 1974.

Medicine Eagle, Brooke: *Buffalo Woman Comes Singing*; Ballantine Books, New York, 1991.

Meltzer, David; *Birth: An Anthology of Ancient Texts, Songs, Prayers and Stories*; North Point Press, San Francisco, 1981.

Newcomb, Franc J. and Reichard, Gladys A.; *Sandpaintings of the Navajo Shooting Chant*; Dover Pub., New York, 1975.

Roberts, Elizabeth and Amidon, Elias (editors); *Earth Prayers from Around the World: 365 Prayers, Poems and Invocations for Honoring the Earth*; Harper SanFrancisco, San Francisco, 1991.

Starhawk; *The Spiral Dance: A Rebirth of the Ancient Religion of the Great Goddess*; Harper and Row, San Francisco, 1979.

Van Gennup, Arnold; *The Rites of Passage*; University of Chicago Press, Chicago, 1960.

Washbourn, Penelope (editor); *Seasons of Woman: Song, Poetry, Ritual, Prayer, Myth, Story*; Harper and Row, San Francisco, 1979.

NATIVE AMERICAN

Beck, Peggy V.; Walters, Anna Lee; Francisco, Nia; *The Sacred: Ways of Knowledge, Sources of Life*; Navajo Community College/Northland Press, Tsaile & Flagstaff, Arizona, 1990.

Brown, Joseph Epes; *Animals of the Soul: Sacred Animals of the Oglala Sioux*; Element, Rockport, Massachusetts, 1992.

———; The Sacred Pipe: *Black Elk's Account of the Seven Rites of the Oglala Sioux*; Penguin Books, Middlesex, England, 1953.

Halifax, Joan: *Shamanic Voices: A Survey of Visionary Narratives*; E.P. Dutton, New York, 1979.

Highwater, Jamake; *The Primal Mind: Vision and Reality in Indian America*; New American Library, New York, 1981.

Johnson, Sandy and Budnik, Dan; *The Book of Elders: The Life Stories and Wisdom of Great American Indians*; Harper SanFrancisco, San Francisco, 1994.

Margolin, Malcolm (editor); *The Way We Lived: California Indian Reminiscences, Stories and Songs*; Heyday Books, Berkeley, California, 1981.

Moon, Sheila; *A Magic Dwells: A Poetic and Psychological Study of the Navajo Emergence Myth*; Wesleyan University Press, Middletown, Connecticut, 1970.

Neidhart, John G.; *Black Elk Speaks*; Pocket Books, New York, 1932.

———; *When the Tree Flowered: The Story of Eagle Voice, A Sioux Indian*; University of Nebraska Press, Lincoln, Nebraska, 1951.

Rhodes, Robert; *Hopi Music and Dance*; Navajo Community College Press, Tsaile, Arizona, 1977.

Sandner, Donald; *Navajo Symbols of Healing*; Harcourt Brace Jovanovich, New York, 1979.

Spinden, Herbert Joseph; *Songs of the Tewa*; Sunstone Press, Santa Fe, New Mexico, 1993.

Waters, Frank; *Book of the Hopi*; Penguin Books, Middlesex, England, 1963.
———; *Masked Gods*; Ballantine Books, New York, 1950.

INDIGENOUS PEOPLE

Boas, Franz; "Eskimo Tales and Songs", Journal of American Folklore, Vol. 7, Jan/March, 1984.
Bowra, Clarence Maurice; *Primitive Songs*; World Publishing, New York, 1962.
Campbell, Joseph (with Bill Moyers); *The Power of Myth*; Doubleday, New York, 1988.
Chatwin, Bruce; *The Songlines*; Penguin Books, New York, 1987.
Cowan, Tom; *Fire in the Head: Shamanism and the Celtic Spirit*; Harper Collins, New York, 1993.
Estrada, Alvaro; *Maria Sabina: Her Life and Chants*; Ross-Erikson, Santa Barbara, California, 1981.
Feld, Steven; *Sound and Sentiment: Birds Weeping, Poetics and Song in Kaluli Expression*; University of Pennsylvania Press, Philadelphia, 1982.
Lawlor, Robert; *Voices of the First Day: Awakening in the Aboriginal Dreamtime*; Inner Traditions, Rochester, Vermont, 1991.
Lewis, Richard (editor); *I Breathe a New Song: Poems of the Eskimo*; Simon and Schuster, New York, 1971.
Matthews, John; *Taliesin: Shamanism and the Bardic Mysteries in Britain and Ireland*; Aquarian Press, London, 1991.
Roberts, Helen and Jennes, Diamond; "Songs of the Copper Eskimo"; Report of the Canadian Arctic Expedition 1913-1918, Vol.14, F. A. Auckland, Ottawa, 1925.
Sproul, Barbara C.; *Primal Myths: Creating the World*; Harper and Row, San Francisco, 1979.
Suzuki, David and Knudtson, Peter; *Wisdom of the Elders*; Bantam Books, New York, 1992.
Van der Post, Laurens; *The Heart of the Hunter: Customs and Myths of the African People*; Harcourt Brace Jovanovich, New York, 1961.
———; *The Lost World of the Kalahari*; Harcourt Brace Jovanovich, New York, 1958.

Bibliography

Von Franz, Marie-Louise; *Creation Myths*; Spring Publications, Zurich, Switzerland, 1975.

Wentz, W. Y. Evans; *The Fairy-Faith in Celtic Countries*; Humanities Press, Highlands, New Jersey, 1978.

CONSCIOUSNESS

Angelo, Jack; *Spiritual Healing: Energy Medicine for Today*; Element Books, Rockport, Massachusetts, 1991.

Bancroft, Ann; *Origins of the Sacred*; Arkana, London,1987.

Edinger, Edward; *Anatomy of the Psyche*; Open Court, La Salle, Illinois, 1985.

Grof, Stanislav; *Realms of the Human Unconsciousness: Observations from LSD Research*; E.P. Dutton, New York, 1967.

Harding, M. Esther; *Psychic Energy: It's Source and It's Transformation*; Princeton University Press, Princeton, New Jersey, 1963.

Jung, C. G.; *Memories, Dreams and Reflections*; Vintage Books, New York, 1965.

———; *The Archetypes of the Collective Unconscious*, Volume 9; Princeton University Press, Princeton, New Jersey, 1963.

Larsen, Stephen; *The Mythic Imagination*; Bantam Books, New York, 1990.

Levine, Steven; *Who Dies?*; Anchor Press/Doubleday, Garden City, New York, 1982.

Progoff, Ira; *Jung, Synchronicity and Human Destiny: Noncausal Dimensions of Human Experience*; Delta Books, New York, 1973.

———; *The Symbolic and the Real*; McGraw-Hill, New York, 1963.

Samples, Bob; *The Metaphoric Mind*; Addison-Wesley Publishing, Reading, Massachusetts, 1976.

Watkins, Mary; *Waking Dreams*; Harper Colophon, New York, 1976.

Watson, Lyall; *Lifetide*; Bantam Books, New York, 1979.

Wilbur, Ken; *The Spectrum of Consciousness*; Theosophical Publishing House, Wheaton, Illinois, 1977.

———; *Up From Eden: A Transpersonal View of Human Evolution*; Shambhala, Boulder, Colorado, 1983.

LITERATURE

Angelou, Maya; *I Know Why the Caged Bird Sings*; Virago, London, 1984.

———; *Singing and Swingin' and Gettin' Merry Like Christmas*; Virago, London, 1985.

———; *All God's Children Need Traveling Shoes*; Vintage Books, New York, 1986.

Bly, Robert; *Silence in the Snowy Fields*; Wesleyan University Press, Middletown, Connecticut, 1962.

Bly, Robert, Hillman, James, and Meade, Michael (editors); *The Rag and Bone Shop of the Heart: Poems for Men*; Harper Perennial, New York, 1993.

Boer, Charles (translation); *The Homeric Hymns*; Swallow Press, Chicago, 1970.

Card, Orson Scott; *Songmaster*; Tom Doherty Associates, New York, 1987.

García Lorca, Federico; *The Gypsy Ballads (trans. Rolfe Humphries)*; Indiana University Press, Bloomington, 1953.

——— ; *Poems of Federico García Lorca (trans. Paul Blackburn)*; Momo's Press, San Francisco, 1979.

——— ; *Deep Song and Other Prose (trans. Christopher Maurer)*; New Directions, New York, 1980.

——— ; *The Cricket Sings (trans. Will Kirkland)*; New Directions, New York, 1980.

Hogart, R.C. (translation); *The Hymns of Orpheus*; Phanes Publishing, Grand Rapids, Michigan, 1993.

LeSueur, Meridel; *Rites of Ancient Ripening*, Vanilla Press, Minneapolis, 1975.

McCaffrey, Ann; *Dragon Song*; Bantam Books, New York, 1977.

——— ; *Dragon Singer*; Bantam Books, New York, 1978.

——— ; *Dragondrums*; Bantam Books, 1980.

Montgomery, Stuart; *Circe*; Fulcrum Press, London, 1969.

Morrison, Toni; *Beloved*; Chatto and Windus, London, 1987.

Rilke, Rainer Maria; *Sonnets to Orpheus (trans. MacIntyre, C.F.)*; Norton, New York, 1967.

Rothenberg, Jerome; *Technicians of the Sacred*; Anchor/Doubleday, New York, 1969.

——— ; *Shaking the Pumpkin;* University of New Mexico Press, Albuquerque, New Mexico, 1992.
Shange, Ntozake; *for colored girls who have considered suicide/ when the rainbow is enuf*; Bantam Books, New York, 1980.
Snyder, Gary; *Earth House Hold*; New Directions, New York, 1969.
——— ; *The Old Ways*; City Lights, San Francisco, 40077.
——— ; *The Real Work: Interviews & Talks 1964~1979*; New Directions, New York, 1980.
——— ; *The Practice of the Wild: Essays*; North Point Press, Berkeley, 1990.
Walker, Alice; *Meridian*; The Women's Press, London, 1982.
——— ; *The Color Purple*; The Women's Press, London, 1983.
——— ; *The Temple of My Familiar*; Pocket Books, New York, 1989.

ARTICLES

Brodsky, Warren and Niedorf, Hannah ; "Songs From the Heart: New Paths to Greater Maturity"; The Arts in Psychotherapy, Volume 13, 1986, pp. 333-341.
Densmore, David; "Speaking of Singing"; The New Times, 1988.
Dossey, Larry; "The Body as a Melody"; Magical Blend Magazine, 1991, pp. 47-49.
Hale, Susan Elizabeth; "The Woman Who Had No Voice"; Hembra: A Journal of Southwest Feminist Thought, Volume 2, No. 10, p. 5.
Hale, Susan Elizabeth; "Sitting on Memory's Lap"; The Arts in Psychotherapy, 1990, Volume 17, pp. 269-274.
Hale, Susan Elizabeth; "Wounded Woman: The Use of Guided Imagery and Music in Recovering From a Mastectomy"; Journal of the Association for Music and Imagery, Volume 1, 1992, pp. 99-106.
McAllester, David P.; "Coyote's Song"; Parabola, Volume V, No. 2, 1982, pp. 47-51.
McClelland, Jean; "Freeing Your Natural Voice"; Nature and Health, 1987, pp. 21-23.

Pittman, Lillian; "What Woman Has Breasts Like That?"; The Crone Chronicles, 1992, pp. 12-13.
Sagel, Jim; "New Songs, Young Feet Carry On Ancient Messages"; Albuquerque Journal, February 25, 1987.
Sataloff, Robert T.; "The Human Voice"; Scientific American, 1992, pp. 108-115.
Veldhuis, Hollace Anne; "Spontaneous Songs of Preschool Children"; The Arts in Psychotherapy, Volume 11, 1984, pp. 15-24.

Bibliography

RECORDINGS

Voices: A Compilation of the World's Greatest Choirs
presented through Joachim-Ernst Berendt

available through: YES! Bookshop Catalog
1035 31st Street NW
Washington, D.C. 20007

Basic Vocal Technique taught by Penny Nichols

Learn to Yodel taught by Cathy Fink and Tod Whitemore

Learning to Sing Harmony taught by Cathy Fink, Marcy Marxer, Robin and Linda Williams

Singing in the African American Tradition: Choral and Congregational Vocal Music taught by Ysaye M. Barnwell with George Brandon

available through: Homespun Tapes
PO Box 694
Woodstock, New York 12498

All For Freedom
I Got Shoes
In This Land
Still On the Journey
Sweet Honey in the Rock

available through: Music For Little People
PO Box 1460
Redway, California 95560

Voices of Forgotten Worlds Audio and Book Collection

available through: Signals Catalog
WGBH Educational Foundation
PO Box 64428
St. Paul, Minnesota 55164

Enriching Your Natural Voice taught by Jean McClelland

available through: Jean McClelland
PO Box 2281
New York, New York 10108

Visions Speaking
A Gift of Song
Singing Joy to the Earth
For My People
Brooke Medicine Eagle

available through: Harmony Network
PO Box 2550
Guerneville, California 95446

Susan
Susan Osborn
Concert for the Earth
Missa Gaia/Earth Mass
Common Ground
Paul Winter Consort

available through: Earth Music Productions
PO Box 68
Litchfield, Connecticut 06759

Healing Yourself with Your Own Voice taught by Don Campbell
Drink From the Well: How to Reclaim Your Natural Voice by Michele George
Vocal Awareness: How to Discover Nature and Project Your Natural Voice taught by Arthur Joseph (five tapes and workbook)
Chant: The Healing Power of Voice and Ear with Tim Wilson
The World Sings Goodnight: Lullabies of 33 Cultures in their Native Tongues
Soundings: Spiritual Songs from Many Traditions

Recordings

available through:

Sounds True Catalog
735 Walnut Street, Dept. SC91
Boulder, Colorado 80302
800-333-9185

Circle the Earth with Song
Sacred Ground
Susan Elizabeth Hale

available through:

Susan Elizabeth Hale
PO Box 777
Sandia Park, New Mexico, 87047

Finding Your Voice
Loosen Up and Improvise
Rhiannon

available through:

Ladyslipper Catalog
(catalog of womens' music)
PO Box 3124
Durham, North Carolina 27715
800-634-6044

For other interesting recordings:

Heartsong Review
(quarterly catalog with many titles)
PO Box 1084
Cottage Grove, Oregon 97424

VIDEOS

Singing for Tin Ears taught by Penny Nichols
Vocal Style and Performance: Tips From a Pro
taught by Maria Muldaur
Vocalist's Guide to Fitness, Health and Musicianship
taught by Julie Lyonn Lieberman

available through: Homespun Tapes
PO Box 694
Woodstock, New York 12498

Sing Along Songs Volume I~II; Walt Disney Home Video

Willie the Operatic Whale; Walt Disney Mini Classics Video

The Little Mermaid; Walt Disney Home Video

The Songs Are Free with Bernice Johnson Reagon
Amazing Grace with Bill Moyers

available through: Mystic Fire Video
PO Box 2249
Livonia, Michigan 48151

Canyon Consort with The Paul Winter Consort
(Live in the Grand Canyon)

available through: Living Music Records
65G Gate 5
Sausalito, California 94965

Resources

THROAT CARE

Open Throat

1.) When singing make sure your head and neck are in alignment. Imagine a string attached to the top of your head gently pulling your neck towards the sky.
2.) Imitate the sounds that little puppies make when they're whimpering.
3.) Practice feeling coolness in the back of the throat. Imagine you've just eaten a peppermint candy and you see a friend you haven't seen in years. Let out a surprised "AHHHHHHH".

Folk Remedies

Ginger tea— place 3 slices of raw ginger per cup of tea in boiling water. Let this sit for five minutes. This tea is very warming and especially good in cold weather.
Ginger/honey hot lemonade— Add water to 3 slices of ginger, half a lemon, one tablespoon of honey. Boil water for one minute. Let this sit for five minutes. Drink hot.

Self-Massage

Massage your face and neck with slow, firm motions.
Move your tongue around in your mouth. Stick out your tongue and extend it as far as you can.
Make airplane engine sounds with your lips.
Remember that you sing with the whole body and not just with the throat.
Massage yourself around the abdomen and diaphragm area.

Other Tips

Whenever possible express your feelings through words or sounds. The voice is like a pressure valve to release emotions and allow them to move through so they don't get stuck in the body.

If your throat is sore or tired, allow it to be quiet and relaxed.
Be gentle with yourself!

The voice is delicate and responds to changes in weather, diet, sleep, stress, and illness.

In cold weather protect your neck and throat by wearing a warm scarf.
Please take good care of yourself!

Drink lots of water.

Tone and sing everyday.

Resources

ADDRESSES

American Association for Music Therapy
66 Morris Avenue, PO Box 359
Springfield, New Jersey 07081

Chalice of the Repose Project
St. Patrick Hospital Chalice
554 West Broadway
Missoula, Montana 59806

Guided Imagery and Music Trainings
Association for Music and Imagery
331 Soquel Avenue, Suite 201
Santa Cruz, California 95062

Institute for Music, Health and Education
PO Box 1244
Boulder, Colorado 80306

International Center for the Dances of Universal Peace
444 N.E. Ravenna Blvd., Suite 306
Seattle, Washington 98115

National Association for Music Therapy, Inc.
8455 Colesville Road, Suite 930
Silver Springs, Maryland 20910

Joseph Rael
PO Box 1309
Bernalillo, New Mexico 87004

Sound Healers Association
PO Box 2240
Boulder, Colorado 80306

The Tracking Project
John Stokes, Director
PO Box 266
Corrales, New Mexico 87048

Workshops, Song Journeys and Apprenticeships
in the Healing Power of Sound and Song
Susan Elizabeth Hale
PO Box 777
Sandia Park, New Mexico 87047

Colophon

Set in *Adobe Caslon*,
a revitalization by Carol Twombly,
based on the English Baroque type family
designed and cut by William Caslon
in the early 1700's. In this faithful digital version,
one can still find the sculptural fluidity of strokes
& cottage garden air which invites immediate
welcome to the eye & pleases like a catchy tune
whistled while admiring roses.

Book design by J. Bryan

Susan Elizabeth Hale,
MA, MT-BC, ATR,
is a singer, songwriter, poet, and performance artist.
She lives on the east side
of Oku-pin—*Turtle Mountain*.